Regulating Traffic Safety

Y0-BVO-566

Regulating Traffic Safety

Martin Friedland
Michael Trebilcock
Kent Roach

UNIVERSITY OF TORONTO PRESS
Toronto Buffalo London

© University of Toronto Press 1990
Toronto Buffalo London
Printed in Canada

ISBN 0-8020-6764-6

Printed on acid-free paper

Canadian Cataloguing in Publication Data

Friedland, M. L. (Martin Lawrence), 1932–
    Regulating traffic safety

    Also published in: Securing compliance:
    seven case studies
    ISBN 0-8020-6764-6

    1. Traffic safety. 2. Traffic regulations.
    I. Trebilcock, Michael J., 1941–   .
    II. Roach, Kent, 1961–   .
    III. Title.

    HE5614.F73 1990   363.12'56   C90-093832-3

Contents

Preface

This manuscript also forms part of a separately published volume of studies, *Securing Compliance: Seven Case Studies* (Toronto: University of Toronto Press, 1990). The subjects in that volume range from securities regulation and prostitution to environmental protection and family violence. Also included there are studies of compliance with tax laws and work-place safety as well as this extended analysis of techniques for regulating traffic safety. It was thought that also publishing the traffic safety study in this paperback format would make it more widely available to those with a specific interest in traffic safety.

The Canadian Institute for Advanced Research has made this study possible. Dr Fraser Mustard, president of the institute, has been a constant source of inspiration and encouragement to all of us engaged in the program on sanctions and rewards. Further, the institute's Law and Society Advisory Committee, chaired by David Johnston, principal of McGill University, has also played an important role in helping shape our work.

We are grateful for the valuable research assistance provided by Saskia Oltheten at the early stages of the project and by Neville Austin, Timothy Endicott, Robert Sider, and Jennifer Webster at later stages. Invaluable advice was given to us by a large number of persons on various aspects of the study. We would like to thank, in particular: John Adams, Department of Geography, University of London; Mary Chipman, Department of Preventive Medicine, University of Toronto; Ezra Hauer, Department of Civil Engineering, University of Toronto; Brian Jonah and John Lawson and their colleagues in the federal Department of Transport, Ottawa; Jerry Mashaw and George Priest, of the Yale Law School; Barry Pless, Faculty of Medicine, McGill University; Herb Simpson and his associates, Traffic Injury Research Foundation, Ottawa; Kella Vaga and other members of the Ontario Ministry of Transport and Communications; Evelyn Vingilis, Addiction Research Foundation, Toronto; Norm Wasylyk and other members of the Ontario Provincial Police; and Gerald Wilde, Department of Psychology, Queen's University. Joyce Kawano, Grace Roach, and Kathy Tzimika provided expert secretarial assistance.

Martin Friedland
Michael Trebilcock
Kent Roach
Faculty of Law
University of Toronto

Regulating Traffic Safety

Introduction

We undertook this examination[1] of techniques of controlling traffic accidents as part of a larger study of sanctions and rewards in the legal system.[2] We thought that an understanding of what worked and did not work in the traffic area might give us insights into the regulation of conduct in other fields of law. Traffic accidents were a particularly appropriate focus, we thought, because of the good statistics that we assumed were available and because of the extensive research and other resources that had been and are devoted to the field. We were wrong. The statistics are not particularly good; the effects of various interventions are not well documented; and there is no clear consensus on what works and what does not work. This study outlines some of the techniques of control used to reduce the frequency and severity of traffic accidents, tries to explain why so little is known, and speculates on what approaches may prove most productive.

Most of the effort to control accidents has concentrated on changing driver behaviour, the subject of part I (chapters 1–5). Police surveillance and prosecution have dominated control strategies. But one looks in vain for studies that compare the cost-effectiveness of policing with, for example, road maintenance or specific safety features in cars, the types of environment-centred measures considered in part II (chapters 6–9). Nevertheless, after reviewing the traffic safety literature, our strong impression is that we have concentrated and continue to concentrate our resources too heavily on changing driver behaviour. Switching some of the resources now devoted to policing and prosecutions to improving car and road design and to curtailing activity levels of high-risk classes of drivers would, we believe, improve road safety.

The increasing centrality of the automobile in our lives can be captured by a few suggestive statistics. Table 1 shows the growth in per capita motor vehicle ownership in the United States, the state of New York, and the Canadian province of Ontario from 1930 to 1985.[3] With the constant and dramatic growth in vehicle ownership, the amount driven has, of course, also increased. For example, in Ontario, an estimated 5,600 million kilometres were driven in 1931, compared to an estimated 71,500 million kilometres in 1987.[4] Increased driving has brought with it increased exposure to the risk of automobile accidents, and a recent report on motor vehicle accident compensation in Ontario concluded: 'The social and economic cost of motor vehicle accidents is staggering. In 1986, approximately 6% of Ontario drivers were involved in 187,286 reported motor vehicle accidents; over 100,000 were injured; 1,102 were killed. The average Ontario driver, if licensed at age 16, will drive 650,000 kilometres, become involved in two motor vehicle accidents and be injured in one of them. One in 100 will be killed.'[5] The total number of motor vehicle fatalities in Ontario was 517 in 1930. This number increased fairly consistently over time, peaking in 1973, with 1,959 fatalities, and since that time declining to 1,229 in 1987.[6] American data reveal the same broad trends.[7]

Despite the reality that until the last decade there were increasing aggregate numbers of motor vehicle fatalities, fatality rates have actually dramatically declined in most

TABLE 1
Vehicle registrations per 100 population

	Ontario	New York	USA
1985	60.4	50.2	71.3
1980	63.0	45.6	68.7
1970	39.1	36.8	53.3
1960	33.8	30.2	41.2
1950	24.7	25.2	32.5
1940	18.8	20.6	24.6
1930	16.6	18.5	21.8
1920	7.7	6.5	8.7

industrial countries when the distances driven are considered. For example, in Ontario in 1931, 10.2 people were killed per 100 million kilometres driven; in 1940, 8.6; in 1950, 5.3; in 1960, 4.2; in 1970, 3.2; in 1980, 2.1; in 1987, 1.7.[8] US fatality rates similarly declined from 4.8 people killed per 100 million kilometres driven in 1950 to 3.2 in 1960; 2.9 in 1970; 2.1 in 1980; and 1.6 in 1984.[9] There has been a fairly uniform decrease in fatality rates in many other countries over the years. The OECD in a recent study notes: 'It is remarkable that this uniformity exists in spite of the diversity of legislation, governmental structures, safety programmes and their management.'[10]

Accident and personal injury trends are more ambiguous, in part because problems of reportability (a wish to conceal accidents; changing legal and insurance reportability thresholds) and subjectivity in reporting (by police or traffic personnel) render the data much less reliable. Despite these reservations there were 203,431 reportable accidents, 80,432 personal injury accidents, and 121,089 motor vehicle–related personal injuries in Ontario in 1987.[11] The purely economic costs of motor vehicle accidents in Ontario in 1982 is estimated to be $1.7 billion.[12] In 1987 the estimated property dam-

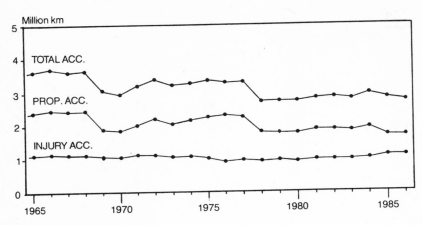

Figure 1
Ontario accident rates: type of accident per million kilometres,
1965–86 (SOURCE: Ministry of Transportation and Communication,
Ontario Road Safety Annual Report)

age caused by motor vehicle accidents was over $680 mil-
lion.[13]

In terms of demand on police and court resources, there
were over 1.2 million convictions under the Ontario Highway Traffic Act in 1987, the vast majority being for speeding.[14] In Canada 128,055 persons were charged with drinking and driving offences, and even though this number
represented an all-time low since data collection began in
1974, it still accounted for one in five persons charged with
any offence under the Criminal Code.[15]

Personal injury and accident rates, per million kilometres
driven, have fallen much less dramatically than fatality
rates; over the past two decades they have remained fairly
constant. These trends are depicted in Figures 1 and 2.[16] The
divergence between fatalities and injuries might permit at
least two explanations: first, while accident frequency has
not declined, accident severity has done so, perhaps reflecting safer vehicles; second, medical science continues to

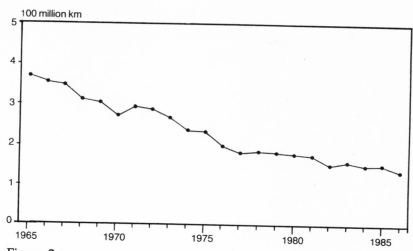

Figure 2
Fatal accident rates in Ontario, per 100 million km, 1965–86
(SOURCE: As for Figure 1, above)

make advances so that many auto-related personal injuries that would once have been fatalities are now non-terminal. Possibly both factors (safer vehicles and improved health care) are at work.

These statistics illustrate that traffic accidents have been an important social problem over the past fifty years. Vast resources have understandably been devoted to the regulation of traffic safety. Let us look at some of the approaches that have been taken to the road safety problem.

A variety of legal interventions were used to regulate the automobile as it was introduced and then popularized. Before automobile fatalities reached significant rates,[17] regulatory patterns were borrowed from the laws applied to horse-drawn carriages. Sanctions were devised, first in Britain and then in Canada, which made the causing of bodily harm by 'wanton or furious driving or racing, or other wilful misconduct, or by wilful neglect'[18] a crime, punishable by up to two years' imprisonment. Likewise, sanctions prohibited reckless driving[19] and drunk driving,[20] first through the use of fines directed against those driving horses, and later by possible terms of imprisonment under the criminal law directed against those driving automobiles.[21] From the start, traffic regulation focused on control of driver behaviour through threat of sanctions.

The prevalence of deterrence strategies of controlling traffic can in part be explained by the automobile's introduction at about the same time as the culmination of a shift in emphasis in methods of policing. Albert Reiss has persuasively shown this 'strategic shift' from inspection and compliance to apprehension and the 'deterrence model of policing.'[22] 'Compliance systems,' he states, 'aim to prevent violations of the law from happening or to reduce their harmful consequences. Deterrence systems must allow violations of the law to occur so that those violations can be punished to produce the deterrent effect.'[23] If the automobile had been introduced earlier and had not been rapidly popularized, its regulation perhaps might have followed the pattern of the regulation of ships and railways, which do not rely primarily on the deterrent effect of criminal prosecutions. For example, both railway companies and unions prohibited their employees from drinking and driving, and it was assumed at the turn of the twentieth century that 'the precaution of railroad companies to have only total abstainers guide their engines will soon extend to the owners and drivers of ... new motor wagons.'[24] If traffic safety regulation had originally been oriented toward compliance as opposed to deterrence, regulation through civil liability and insurance (see chapter 2), licensing (chapter 4), informal systems of sanctions (chapter 1) and rewards (chapter 3), and education (chapter 5) might have played a larger role in traffic regulation than they have done.

Although the compliance technique of licensing was used in the early regulation of traffic safety and some safety advocates called for greater reliance on licensing (as was done in the case of railway engineers subject to compliance-oriented forms of regulation[25]), licensing for automobiles was used mainly to reinforce the criminal process. Provisions were first made in 1901 in New York and in 1903 in both Ontario and Britain[26] for registration of motor vehicles, licensing of drivers, and display of licence plates. Licensing of drivers was used mainly to facilitate imposition of sanctions through identification of offenders who might not stop for the police and also as a means to generate revenue. In many jurisdictions it was often possible to obtain licences through the mail and no tests were given to prospective drivers before they obtained a licence.[27] Revocation and suspension of a driver's licence were provided as a sanction for violations of motoring rules or other misconduct.[28] Licensing techniques were used to sanction identified acts of driver misconduct and not to screen the pool of drivers so as to prevent traffic violations and accidents.

Civil liability has also played a role in regulating traffic safety, but its deterrent effects have been muted by the early availability of motor vehicle insurance. Well into the nineteenth century, it was assumed that a contract for insurance against legal damages would be held void as against the public policy implicit in the court's award of damages.[29] By the time the motor vehicle was popularized at the turn of the twentieth century, however, this belief had eroded and comprehensive motor vehicle insurance was available.[30] The use of insurance to mute the financially disastrous effects of potential third-party civil liability awards is well illustrated in a letter that George Bernard Shaw wrote to a friend in 1913 urging that she obtain insurance against third-party claims 'instantly.'[31]

Insurance against certain third-party claims became compulsory in Massachusetts in 1927 and in Britain in 1930.[32] The effects of these provisions remain largely a matter of conjecture. Under the Massachusetts system, rate-setting apparently became politicized and there was no system of experience rating of individual drivers. At the same time, however, the system may have retained some of the residual deterrent effects of the civil liability system by placing limits on the amount insured.[33] The decline in motorcycle registrations following enactment of the British compulsory insurance law can be related in part to the financial burdens of insurance, which priced impecunious motorcyclists off the road. This use of insurance pricing to reduce activity levels has been called 'an effective means of lowering road deaths' through reducing the proportion of more accident-prone motorcycles in the vehicle fleet.[34] Despite the potential of the civil liability system, even mediated by insurance, to contribute to traffic safety, both the civil liability and insurance systems have become increasingly oriented to compensation rather than to either deterrence or the removal of accident-prone drivers from the road.

In the mid-1930s, highway safety advocates began to focus on driver education as a means to prevent traffic accidents. Accident theory at the time stressed driver irresponsibility as the cause of accidents, but the assumption that driver education would reduce highway injuries and fatalities was never proved. In a 1962 critique of driver education, *The Highway Jungle*, Edward A. Tenney demonstrated a relation between increased enrolment in teenage driver education and increased driving exposure and accidents. The most striking example of the negative effect of driver education was in Michigan. That state won an award in 1960 based on its achieving 100 per cent of its potential enrolment in high school driver education by making education mandatory for licensing but at the same time recorded a 15 per cent increase in traffic fatalities.[35] Despite such evidence, many commentators and policy-makers persisted in believing that driver education could reduce traffic accidents if it increased drivers' safety awareness and responsibility.

For the first fifty years of the motor car, little attention was devoted to such environmental factors as the safety effects of vehicle and road design (see chapters 7 and 8). At an early date, cars were required in Britain and Ontario to use night-time lamps and warning bells in order to prevent accidents.[36] With the exception of some manufacturer concern about the safety of the glass used in windshields, motor vehicles were not designed to lessen the severity of injuries sustained in automobile accidents. In general, manufacturers were more concerned with the cosmetics of annual style changes and the quest for faster, more appealing automobiles than they were with the safety implications of their constant design innovations.[37] Various safety advocates made proposals that the maximum speed of vehicles be reduced by 'gearing down' so that they could not achieve high speeds, but the proposals were universally rejected.[38] Road design, like vehicle design, did not place safety first. The chief concern in the design of roads was cost, durability, the nuisance of dust, and maintenance of traffic flow,[39] not prevention of automobile accidents through, for example, use of controlled access roads or physical separation of pedestrians from automobiles.

Speed limits have from the start been a staple of traffic regulation. Maximum speed limits were first used to discourage automobile travel in the last half of the nineteenth century,[40] but they were used less restrictively with the increasing popularity of motor vehicles. Exact speed limits remained matters for political compromise between advocates of motor cars and groups such as cyclists, pedestrians, and farmers, who disliked 'road hogs' and the use of the motor car in general.[41] Motorist groups, supported by recommendations of two British royal commissions,[42] consistently opposed speed limits and suggested that laws against dangerous driving be more rigorously enforced[43] and 'danger zones' requiring 'special caution' be marked.[44] Maximum speed limits outside towns were even abolished in Britain and in some Canadian and American jurisdictions, for a period in the 1930s,[45] but the safety effects of these changes are far from clear.

Before the 1960s almost all traffic safety regulation had been directed at influencing the behaviour of the driver and preventing[46] crashes – the focus of part I. Depending on the interests of the advocate, most accidents were attributed to human error and irresponsibility by either drivers or pedestrians or simply acts of God.[47] Most people believed that improvement in driver performance was needed to reduce traffic accidents, and there was considerable reluctance to focus on either the vehicle or the roadway environment as a cause of accidents or even as a means to regulate traffic safety.[48] Criminal sanctions against dangerous, careless, or drunken behaviour of drivers were the most popular forms of control, but speed limits, licence suspensions, driver education, civil liability, and the operation of insurance markets were also used to influence the behaviour of drivers.

Starting in the late 1950s, attention was no longer exclusively focused on drivers' care levels and the prevention of crashes, as traffic safety experts and eventually policy-makers began to realize that the damage sustained in crashes could be reduced by other forms of environmental regulation – the focus of part II. Physicians and researchers began to study the ways in which injuries, as opposed to accidents, could be prevented and reduced. At this time they proposed use of seat-belts to decelerate the body within the vehicle and lessen the consequences of what became known as the 'second collision.' They also criticized auto manufacturers for making cars with interiors and exteriors that were unforgiving to humans upon collision.[49] At a political level, consumer groups eagerly embraced the criticisms of automobile design,[50] and policy-makers became sceptical of the traditional focus on driving behaviour and looked increasingly to new forms of public regulation that they hoped would reduce, even cure, 'the highway epidemic' in the same scientific manner as many public health problems such as tuberculosis and typhoid had been overcome through centralized regulation.[51] The culmination of these intellectual and political trends occurred in 1966, when the US Congress introduced a comprehensive, centralized regulatory framework for automobile design.[52] A new era in traffic safety had begun, influenced in large part by accident analysis, which stressed regulation of automobile safety (see chapter 7) and highway design (chapter 8), not control of driving behaviour, to reduce both the frequency and the severity of accidents.

The intellectual foundation for the new focus on the safety effects of automobile and environmental design came primarily from the work of William Haddon, Jr, who as an epidemiologist advanced a conceptual framework (the Haddon matrix) that provided a new way of analysing automobile accidents and the various methods of reducing their costs; as a policy-maker he headed the first American agency with a comprehensive mandate to regulate traffic safety.[53] The Haddon matrix continues to provide the analytic framework for much continued research in traffic safety.[54] This matrix distinguishes human, vehicle, and environmental factors in accidents and temporally breaks down accidents into pre-crash, crash, and post-crash phases for analysing potential interventions. These categories had their origins in the traditional epidemiological terms of host (in this case, those injured in motor vehicle accidents), agent (mechanical energy of the vehicle), and environment (the vehicle and surroundings in which the host and agent interact). Haddon argued that attention should be paid to all three factors, because automobile accidents represented 'a straightforward example of the epidemiologic triad: the host – the person susceptible to injury – interacts with the necessary, specific agent – mechanical energy – and with the en-

TABLE 2
Haddon matrix

	Human	Vehicles and equipment	Environment (physical)	Environment (socio-cultural)
Pre-crash	Driver education, licensing, prohibitions against speeding, careless and drunk driving	Motor vehicle design standards (e.g. centre-mounted brake light), lower speed capacities in vehicles	Roadsigns, highway design, separation of pedestrians from vehicles by walkways and barriers	Taxation of fuel and cars, minimum drinking and driving ages, liquor control regulation
Crash	Use of motorcycle helmets and seat-belts	Designing interiors to reduce the effects of the second collision, i.e. collapsible steering wheels, padded dashes, resistant windshields, head rests, automatic seat-belts and airbags	Barriers that gradually decelerate the vehicle	Attitudes toward seat-belt usage
Post-crash	Limiting access of the most vulnerable people in this phase to licences (e.g. the aged and haemophiliacs), requirements to stop and provide assistance after an accident	Fire-resistant fuel tanks, regulation of the repair industry	Roadside emergency telephones and access for emergency vehicles	Emergency health care service and rehabilitation efforts

vironment – the impacted structure, and the interacting characteristics of all three determine whether the specific pathology, that is, mechanical-energy-exchange injury, occurs and with what timing, characteristics, and severity.'[55] The matrix, with concrete examples of various interventions, is presented in Table 2, but we shall first outline the intellectual perspective that Haddon and his fellow epidemiologists brought to the study of traffic safety.

The epidemiologists imposed on traffic safety a vast store of knowledge accumulated from study of the control of infectious diseases and a scientific perspective that dismissed 'the unscientific term "accident" with its connotations of chance, fate and unexpectedness.'[56] Failures in human performance were bound to occur, and 'the design of any system should be based on expectations of minimum levels of human performance.'[57] Some automobile crashes were inevitable, and Haddon criticized current traffic safety measures, almost all aimed at driver behaviour in the pre-crash phase, for their preoccupation with human factors and with reducing the incidence of crashes. Greater attention to the injury-producing effects of the vehicle and crash environment could prove the most effective means to reduce the harmful results of automobile accidents as measured by injuries and deaths.

The epidemiologists' concern with injury led them to concentrate on the effects of the 'second collision,' as energy is released with the abrupt deceleration of a vehicle's occupants within the vehicle upon collision. They sought, wherever possible, to limit the energy created and to spread deceleration forces over space and time in order to avoid harmful levels of energy release that would result in injury.[58] Their policy prescriptions concentrated on the accident environment as the most effective target for collective and centralized regulation and devoted less attention to the prevention of individual error and the assignment of individual blame.[59]

The new injury-control perspective challenged traditional legal interventions based on concepts of fault, negligence, and individual responsibility. For example, even in a case of an accident involving a driver who is drunk, epidemiologists refuse to concentrate solely on impairment of driving skills but also explore environmental factors that contribute to injury.[60] They ask the question: why did the roadway environment become too challenging for the drunk driver at the particular location of the accident? Could the injuries sustained in the alcohol-related accident have been prevented or reduced in severity by safer vehicle design and better post-crash treatment (see chapter 9)? In their efforts to discover the most effective means to reduce injuries, epidemiologists were willing to accept human (mis)behaviour as a given and avoided moralistic approaches to public health problems.

Haddon re-evaluated the significance of the search for primary causal factors which were the premise for most findings of criminal or civil liability. The discovery or prevention of the proximate cause of accidents was not likely to be the most efficient means to prevent the harm. Haddon maintained:

> The choice of countermeasures should *not* be determined by the relative importance of causal or contributing factors or by their early occurrence in the sequence of injury-producing events ... Rather priority and emphasis should be given to the measures that will *most effectively* reduce losses from injury. As a result of failure to understand this point emphasis on human error as the cause of most injuries has resulted in undue emphasis on changing behaviour, rather than on using more effective measures to reduce injuries and their results.[61]

Causal analysis had encouraged policy-makers to concentrate on the most overt cause of damage and ignore the basic epidemiological insight that injury was the result of the necessary interaction of agent, environment, and host and that a change in any one factor could prevent or reduce the severity of injury.[62]

In a traditional legal framework, much energy is devoted to isolating and punishing blameworthy behaviour,[63] whereas in the epidemiological framework, attention is devoted to whatever source will be most effective in reducing injuries and their harmful consequences. Epidemiological research has been characterized by general scepticism about the effectiveness of trying to change the levels of care that individuals adopt in potentially hazardous activities, although in recent years there has been increased interest in examining the interaction between behavioural and environmental determinants of injuries.[64]

The epidemiological approach to motor vehicle accidents should be seen as a framework that expands the possibilities and scope of legal regulation rather than one that entirely rejects the efficacy of traditional legal sanctions directed at driver behaviour. The adaptation[65] of the Haddon matrix in Table 2 illustrates that each cell can be a locus for legal regulation, imposition of sanctions, and offering of rewards. The symmetry of the matrix should not confuse policy-makers into assuming that interventions in each cell could be equally effective in reducing injuries. As we have discussed, Haddon himself was most optimistic about the possibility of regulation of the vehicle-crash phase.[66]

Haddon and other epidemiologists have often been perceived as advocates for passive strategies such as airbags which are centred in the vehicle-crash phase. Their policy proposals reflect in part a desire to overcome historical neglect of the crash phase as well as scepticism about the possibilities of changing the behaviour of individuals on a large scale. Haddon compared the active strategy of influencing people to wear seat-belts to the passive strategy of regulating airbags. Airbags and seat-belts both attenuate the potentially damaging energy transfer that occurs with sudden deceleration, but the active approach of seat-belts requires, 'for complete success, billions of individual actions per month by all sorts of people in all sorts of mental and physiological states. On the other hand, the universal provision of airbags to achieve the same purpose would require only a single behaviour change. A simple binding decision by one federal official or by some three or four executives of motor vehicle manufacturing companies.'[67] Haddon insisted that the active approach of encouraging seat-belt use through sanctions and education and the passive approach of requiring automatic restraints through regulation were 'compatible and complementary,'[68] but he made it clear that over the broad range of injuries and diseases, preventive passive approaches had enjoyed more success than active approaches, which require widespread changes in the behaviour of individuals.[69]

The Haddon matrix and the epidemiological approach to injury control have been influential in conceptualizing the social problem of automobile accidents and the damage they create. Despite resurgence in concerns about regulating the behaviour of drivers and stressing individual responsibility, a prestigious panel recently appointed by the US National Research Council concluded that the most effective and promising manner of reducing injury was through product and environmental design. Such design, once in place, provides automatic protection without the manipulation of mass behaviour through the widespread use of sanctions, rewards, or education.[70]

A major analytical challenge to the epidemiological perspective that treats driver behaviour more or less as given and stresses changes to the accident environment has emerged over the last decade or so and is discussed in chapter 7. This challenge rejects the notion that road users should be viewed as passive agents in the traffic environment and argues instead that road users are likely to adapt their behaviour in response to changes in that environment.

This competing perspective was brought into prominence through a controversial article published in 1975 by University of Chicago economist Sam Peltzman,[71] who argued, on the basis of empirical analysis, that motor vehicle safety design improvements mandated under the US National Traffic and Motor Vehicle Safety Act of 1966 had had no effect on subsequent fatality trends: 'The one result of this study that can be put forward most confidently is that auto safety regulation has not affected the highway death rate.'[72] Peltzman postulated that by reducing the consequences of the second collision through safety regulations, risk taking, or what he calls 'driving intensity,' would be increased as drivers drove less cautiously in order to achieve the same trade-off that they had experienced prior to regulation between expected accident costs and benefits from conserving time on the road.

In Canada, Gerald Wilde, a Queen's University psychologist, had even earlier developed a theory he called 'risk homeostasis.'[73] Building on the work of a psychologist[74] who had shown that galvanic skin responses (indicating levels of anxiety) remained more or less the same under various driving conditions, Wilde developed a theory that all safety improvements are used up by the population as a whole in riskier driving. The homeostasis theory was to a considerable extent subsequently adopted by John Adams[75] of the University of London (see chapter 1 – re seat-belt usage – and 8) and has been the subject of vigorous debate in the literature.[76]

We accept that there will be some adaptive behaviour in drivers to safety features. Studies that show, for example, that drivers with studded tires take curves on icy surfaces faster than drivers without such tires[77] are not surprising. One tends to speed up when road conditions are good and slow down in poor weather or when one's brakes are not working properly. But many safety improvements, such as collapsible steering wheels, safety glass, and stronger side-

door beams, are not known or only imperfectly appreciated
and so do not generate immediate feedback to the driver. So
there is not likely to be much, if any, compensation in these
cases. Moreover, as we will see in the discussion of seat-
belts, it is unlikely that drivers will increase their driving
risks just because they are belted. Drivers do not want to
experience an accident, even if it is less severe than it might
otherwise be without being belted. So it is unlikely that
there is any compensation in the case of seat-belts, let alone
homeostasis. The one area where there may be some risk
homeostasis is when drivers are deliberately seeking risks.
Leonard Evans, who argues against risk homeostasis, shows
its applicability to car racing. Although safety keeps improving at the Indianapolis 500, deaths per kilometre travelled
have remained about the same since the race started in 1911;
but speeds have increased from an average of 120 kilo-
metres/hour in 1911 to 263 kilometres/hour in 1984.[78]

Adaptive behaviour – and we believe that it does take
place to some extent[79] – will reduce the potential impact of
safety improvements. Improvements in car safety and road
design cannot deliver quite as much as they promise. The
larger problem, however, lies in the political economy of
safety regulation. Attempts to mandate further safety features in automobile design standards have encountered
much political and legal resistance in the United States.[80]
Given the limitations presented by the problems of political
feasibility and risk compensation, we believe that controlling driving behaviour will still have a role to play in future
traffic safety programs.

An important factor that has brought the use of the criminal law back onto centre stage over the past decade is the
increasing political activity of pressure groups concerned
with victims of drunk driving and the sensitivity of politi-
cians, police, and prosecutors to these groups. This is part of
a growing trend toward concern for victims of crime,[81]
coupled with a move away from rehabilitation toward 'just

deserts' in criminal justice.[82] Whereas in the 1960s collective responsibility for traffic safety was stressed through the epidemiological vision, the 1980s has witnessed a resurgence of attention to the role of driving behaviour and individual responsibility for traffic accidents.

We turn now, in part I, to the various types of interventions, starting with driver-centred counter-measures. We are not convinced that the resources now devoted to enforcement of sanctions to control driving behaviour (for example, speed limits) that may or may not result in accidents is the best use of the resources available for traffic safety programs. We do not advocate abandoning of prosecutions but rather question whether marginal expenditures might not be better spent on non-punitive techniques. As Albert Reiss has stated, 'What seems needed is greater attention to the role that compliance models, which are central to the strategy of regulatory agencies, can contribute to discretionary choices by police managers and their officers.'[83] The area of drunk driving, for example, which will be explored in detail in a later section, would benefit from these mixed strategies of compliance and deterrence. Reiss points out some of the alternatives to arrest for operating a motor vehicle while intoxicated:

> These alternatives include civil suits for damages arising from drunkenness against bartenders who served the intoxicated person, and paying closer attention to whether bar operators are complying with the law regarding the serving of liquor to intoxicated persons. Civil suits and license revocation for violation may be more effective than arrest of intoxicated persons.
> Still other modes of coerced compliance are possible, such as patrolling bars that regularly serve intoxicated persons at late hours. Persons appearing to leave intoxicated who begin to drive may be required to take a sobriety test. Failing the

test might lead to transportation of the intoxicated person to his or her residence or to a detoxification center as well as impounding of the automobile. The cost of impoundment and a graduated set of penalties for recovery of the vehicle associated with repeat offending may be far more effective than simple arrest and incarceration of the offender pending a court appearance.[84]

Just as compliance-based techniques appear preferable to over-reliance on deterrence-based sanctions, so an epidemiological approach, concentrating on environmental factors and taking driving behaviour largely as a given, may prove more effective in many cases than reliance on efforts to change driving behaviour. We also emphasize the often-neglected potential for major reductions in traffic accidents from exposure-limiting counter-measures through licensing and pricing systems.

PART ONE

Driver-Centred Counter-measures

1
Sanctions

Prosecutions are today the most prominent policy instrument used to reduce traffic accidents. Apart from Criminal Code prosecutions, there have been over a million convictions under the Highway Traffic Act each year in Ontario for the past ten years.[85] Traffic offences consume a large proportion of police and court resources. A recent British document estimated that road traffic offences occupied 'between 50% and 70% of Magistrates' court time.'[86] The same may well be true for lower court judges in Canada.[87] This concentration of resources on prosecutions in the traffic area raises the question of whether they are effective in controlling the conduct of drivers and, more important, whether this then leads to fewer accidents.

Most Highway Traffic Act offences are based primarily on the concept of deterrence. This appears to be true in most common law jurisdictions. 'Deterrence is in many ways the most important objective of road traffic safety,' states the 1988 *British Road Traffic Law Review Report Document*.[88]

Deterrence comes in two different forms – general and specific (or special) deterrence. Specific deterrence refers to the impact on a specific individual of a penalty or a potential penalty directed against that individual. General deterrence refers to the impact of a penalty or a potential penalty on others. Both may be operative in a particular case. A person may be subject to deterrence by a sentence he or she had personally received as well as by knowledge of how others have been dealt with. Deterrence is wider than the fear of state-administered punishment, and many writers advocate that it be understood to include such factors as the stigma of arrest, the jeopardizing of relationships, and the effect of the sanction on future personal goals.[89]

Deterrence can operate even if the persons on whom it is to operate have limited rather than full rationality. As economist Philip Cook states: 'The existence of a strong deterrent effect does not require that potential criminals be fully informed or fully rational in their crime decisions ... The prediction that crime is deterrable follows just as readily from an assumption that 10 per cent of criminals are capable of rational decision-making as from an assumption that all potential criminals have that ability.'[90] The more rational the actor, the more he or she will be influenced by potential penalties. Virtually everyone has violated the traffic code at one time or another. Thus the traffic offender reflects the general population more than many other classes of offenders do and so is toward the higher end of a rationality scale.

To what extent does deterrence work? There are two separate questions that must be examined. The first is whether prosecutions can affect the conduct prohibited. The second and more important is whether deterrence affects the accident rate.

No doubt traffic offenders are deterred by the prospect of prosecutions. Most of us slow down when we see a police cruiser at the side of the road and think twice about parking illegally if the potential penalty is relatively high. As the Canadian Sentencing Commission confidently stated in its recent report: 'The weight of the evidence and the exercise of common sense favour the assertion that, taken together, legal sanctions have an overall deterrent effect which is difficult to evaluate precisely.'[91] But, how long will deterrence last? Will people speed up again when the police cruiser has been passed, and will they continue to park illegally when the anti-parking blitz has ended? Are there better techniques for controlling conduct than criminal prosecutions?

Although the criminal sanction is the principal weapon used to prevent traffic accidents, there is real doubt about its effectiveness in relation to accidents. Would the number of accidents increase if there were no enforcement? Certainly the number of traffic citations would go down, but would accidents go up? A 1980 study in Tennessee measured accidents during a police slowdown that followed a period of high enforcement.[92] Its conclusion was as follows: 'The present retrospective analysis of police traffic enforcement shows that wide variations in the overall levels of enforcement have no immediate measurable impact on the frequency or severity of traffic accidents.'[93]

A police slowdown in Metropolitan Toronto in 1985 as a result of a labour dispute warrants more careful investigation than we were able to give to it. In spite of the fact that convictions under the Highway Traffic Act went down from 476,938 in 1984 to 259,767 in 1985,[94] the number of fatalities remained about the same: 97 in 1984 and 98 in 1985. However, personal injury accidents went up from 15,325 in 1984 to 17,667 in 1985. A full study of accidents during police slowdowns would give useful insights on the relationship between enforcement and accidents. Did the accident rate rise, for example, after the *Toronto Star*'s banner headline of January 13, 1988: 'Police vote to stop issuing tickets'?

A Transport Canada study conducted in Toronto in 1973[95] looked at the effect of varying levels of police enforcement on driver behaviour and safety at a number of urban intersections. The results cast doubt on the effect of police visibility, finding that while there is an immediate reduction in the number of violations committed by motorists they revert to their earlier patterns when increased enforcement ceases.[96] Moreover, the violations most affected by the presence of the police tend to be those of low severity (e.g. signalling a turn) in terms of safety risk,[97] compared to the serious risk involved in running a red light. Further, total accidents during the month of increased enforcement were higher than in any other month during the previous or subsequent year. One possible explanation put forward was that police presence encouraged the reporting of accidents.[98] In another study, John Gardiner examined traffic law enforcement in four cities in Massachusetts in the 1960s and found wide variations in enforcement policies. His conclusion was that 'no evidence was found to support the theory either that high ticketing will produce a low accident rate ... or that high accident rates will cause the police to adopt a strict ticketing policy.'[99]

These studies would lead one to view prosecutions with some caution as a technique of control. However, sanctions cannot be too quickly dismissed as a control technique. The very existence of a law, as we will see in the discussion of seat-belts, will have a positive effect on compliance, and, as in the case of drinking and driving, the raising of potential penalties may affect attitudes toward the conduct in question. Moreover, some enforcement will further increase levels of compliance by raising the perception of the chance of being caught. Certainly courts believe in the deterrent effect of enforcement. In a recent judgment of the Supreme Court of Canada dealing with the legality of a roadside screening device to detect drunk drivers, Mr Justice Le Dain stated for the court: 'The most effective deterrent is the strong possibility of detection.'[100] The question is, how much enforcement is desirable and will the answer vary from subject area to subject area? Let us turn to some of the issues connected with sanctions.

One key question is whether it is better to increase the severity of punishments or the rate of prosecution. Increasing certainty of apprehension would seem to be proportionately better than increasing severity of sanctions, both when the punishment is in the form of imprisonment and also when the punishment is a fine.[101] With respect to imprisonment, Philip Cook points out that two years in prison would not seem to be twice as bad to the average person as one year's imprisonment. Similarly, laboratory experiments show that people make the choice, if given a choice, of a smaller probability of a proportionately larger fine rather than the converse.[102] A recent study surveyed a sample of about 750 persons in 1982 in Baltimore and reached the same conclusion.[103] Various fact situations and consequences were put to those surveyed for a response. The authors concluded that, for predatory crime (e.g. armed robbery, selling drugs, embezzlement), 'increasing the likelihood of a criminal conviction and criminal sanction is likely to be more effective than lengthening prison sentences under a deterrence based punishment scheme.'[104] Most persons, it seems, are more concerned about the present than the future.

Even if increasing the penalty were in theory more effective than increasing the number of prosecutions, it might not be a cost-effective approach, because the higher the penalty, the more inclined a person will be to contest a prosecution. This could result in a greater number of trials and greater court congestion and thus greater cost to society. To avoid these results the police might become reluctant to charge persons, the Crown more willing to plea bargain, and the courts more reluctant to impose higher sentences.[105] Moreover, too high a penalty (to compensate for a small number of convictions) could be considered unfair by many citizens,[106] with resulting disrespect for the law, and might be struck down by the courts as 'cruel and unusual' punishment.[107] In a recent Supreme Court of Canada case,[108] Mr Justice Lamer stated that although the judge or the legislator can consider general deterrence that goes beyond the particular offender, 'the resulting sentence must not be grossly disproportionate to what the offender deserves.' Further, making the penalty too high would overdeter people (e.g. they might drive too slowly or not at all)[109] and could undermine the effectiveness of marginal deterrence (the imposition of increased penalties for acts of increased severity) to help deter engagement in the more serious conduct.[110] However, increasing the number of convictions requires more police officers and tends to reduce the stigma of conviction. Finding the right balance between certainty and severity is one of the most important issues in the use of deterrence strategies.

A further issue that is raised in the literature[111] is the question of celerity, that is, whether swiftness of punishment has a greater deterrent effect than delayed punishment. Certainly the English criminal law in the past believed that speedy justice had the greater deterrent effect. In England in the nineteenth century hangings took place within weeks of the act. Appeals were not permitted in criminal cases in England (with minor exceptions) until 1907. No studies of the effect of 'celerity' in non-laboratory settings[112] have come to light.[113] (The twelve-hour suspension in Ontario for driving with an alcohol level greater than 0.05 is not a true case of the imposition of a punishment, although it may have this effect.)[114] The more delayed a reward, the less of a strengthening effect it has on the behaviour that earned it.[115] The same is no doubt true for sanctions, with respect to both specific and general deterrence.

The target of enforcement, as Christopher Stone suggests,[116] is a further important consideration in deterrence research. Most moving violations under the Highway Traffic Act require that the violator be personally identified and charged.[117] Would compliance be improved if the owner also were subject to prosecution, as he or she is for, say, parking offences? In fairness to the accused, without some proof of guilty knowledge the fine would have to be relatively low[118] and should not be applied to the serious driving offences, but it could apply to moving violations such as speeding and might therefore create additional pressure on the driver. In order to discourage overloading of trucks, a number of American states have made the shipper and the receiver liable to a fine as well as the driver. 'Drivers are pleased to report,' states one safety expert, 'that in these states there is no longer any pressure to take overloads.'[119]

Sanctions usually employed involve fines, imprisonment, or deprivation of licences. Another possible sanction is shame and humiliation, which often accompany a trial. Newspaper publicity, however, can often be very unfair, particularly if the accused is ultimately acquitted. Yet it can be a very effective technique if the severity of the circumstances warrants it.[120] Nigel Walker has suggested that persons convicted of certain serious driving offences could be required to hang a red 'H' or hazard plate on their back licence for a period when they drive, both as a warning to other road users and as a deterrent.[121]

In spite of many studies of deterrence in the past two decades, more research is in fact needed, particularly controlled experiments. Franklin Zimring has pointed out that there are two types of strategies for producing data and insights on deterrence.[122] The first and most common type is cross-sectional or time-series studies, that is, studies that look at crime rates in different jurisdictions or in the same jurisdiction over a period of time and compare penalties imposed and crime rates that occur. However, many factors influence crime rates between jurisdictions and over time, and so it is difficult to determine whether the criminal justice system was responsible for the outcome. Moreover, do a high penalty structure and a low crime rate show that deterrence works, or rather, are the penalties high because the crime is infrequent in the community and viewed as serious by society? Further, an observed effect of an intervention may not result from the intervention but may instead represent regression to a normal pattern (regression to the mean).

This may explain, to take one well-known example, why Governor Ribicoff's tough crackdown on speeding in Connecticut in 1955 by suspension of licences may have seemed to reduce the number of traffic deaths in the state: the number was simply artificially high in the previous year.[123]

A more promising approach, as identified by Zimring, is to study 'the impact of changes in law enforcement or punishment policy by closely following what happens after particular policy shifts occur.'[124] There have been fewer of these studies. The Kansas City Preventative Patrol Experiment,[125] in which intensive preventive police patrolling was increased in certain areas of the city, and the Minneapolis Spousal Violence Study,[126] in which various forms of police intervention in domestic violence disputes were studied, are examples of this second, more promising approach.

A combination of research strategies might prove the most effective. Perhaps one of the best methods of studying deterrence is to examine by a time-series analysis the effects of specific legislative or other changes within one jurisdiction, in comparison to another jurisdiction that has not undergone the same changes.

No doubt the best method would be directly to control variables, but this would require that the courts and the police be involved in setting up control groups, and the courts and, to a lesser extent, the police would have serious reservations about doing so.

To what extent does the current state of knowledge suggest that deterrence works in relation to three specific areas: seat-belts, speed limits, and drunk driving?

Sanctions and Seat-belt Use

Seat-belt use varies widely from one jurisdiction to another. It therefore provides a natural laboratory for examining variations in the law and in police and other practices and their likely effect on rates of compliance as well as on accidents and injuries. An understanding of wide variations within and between jurisdictions in seat-belt use may give us more general insights into the deterrent force of the law.

Ontario was the first jurisdiction in North America to pass a law making seat-belt use compulsory. The law, passed in December 1975,[127] came into force on 1 January 1976. It required drivers and passengers in cars equipped with seat-belts to use them. The provincial law had been preceded by a federal law in 1970 requiring installation of belts in all new vehicles.[128] Quebec introduced seat-belt legislation eight months after Ontario. Other provinces followed, and there are now compulsory use laws in all provinces. Alberta and Prince Edward Island introduced their laws on 1 July 1987.

The first US state to have a mandatory use law was New York, which passed its law in December 1985. As of December 1986, twenty-seven states had passed laws and two states had repealed laws previously enacted.[129]

The existence of a seat-belt law will significantly affect seat-belt use.[130] In 1986, provinces with such legislation had a use rate of 67.8 per cent, whereas Alberta and Prince Edward Island had a rate of 27.2 per cent. Although the use rate in non-compulsory jurisdictions had been going up over the years, it was still far below the compulsory use jurisdictions. Lest it be thought that Alberta's rates were low because of 'rugged individualism,' Texas had the highest US rate in 1986. Houston had a use rate of 18 per cent before Texan legislation and is now at almost 70 per cent.[131] And Alberta's rate has risen to 74.3 per cent in 1987, the year after legislation was passed, and to 82.5 per cent in 1988.[132] This supports Jonah and Lawson's claim that use rates are not culturally dictated.[133] Before Ontario introduced its legislation, the use rate, even with considerable propaganda, was below 20 per cent. It went up to 77 per cent after the law was enacted.[134] Nova Scotia's use rate rose from 20 per cent to 80 per cent after legislation in 1985.[135] England's rates remained at about 30 per cent from 1979 to 1982, in spite of large-scale education campaigns which cost approximately £2 million annually.[136] After legislation in 1983, compliance rose to 90 per cent.[137] Repeal of a seat-belt law has an opposite effect. Nebraska repealed its laws, and the usage rate went from 40 per cent to 29 per cent.[138] Switzerland's use went from 30 per cent to 80 per cent when its law was enacted and decreased to 30 per cent when the law was repealed.[139] A recent US survey showed that driver belt use was 48 per cent in selected cities with belt use laws and 30 per cent in cities without such laws.[140] So the existence of a known law, whether or not it is widely enforced, will affect seat-belt use.

What effect will increased enforcement have? The level of enforcement is certainly a factor in causing rates to rise. A number of studies, not surprisingly, have shown that high levels of police activity increase use. Elmira, New York, for example, achieved seat belt use of 80 per cent because of extensive publicity and enforcement.[141] The Elmira program is considered so successful that the National Highway Traffic Safety Administration has funded fifty similar projects.[142]

A similar increase in enforcement activity in the Ottawa area showed a significant increase in usage.[143] During October 1979, there was a tenfold increase in the number of charges laid for non-use of seat belts coupled with publicity about the increased enforcement and public education about seat-belts. Seat-belt use increased from 58 per cent to 80 per cent. (The control city of Kingston remained the same as before.) A similar campaign was successful in Courtenay, British Columbia,[144] and as a result a province-wide effort was launched during the spring of 1983 which caused seat-belt use to rise from 58 per cent to 73 per cent across the province.[145] What is the long-term effect of these enforcement efforts? The 1986 figures show British Columbia to be still very high at 78 per cent. The 80 per cent rate in Ottawa dropped to 77 per cent after one month and to 70 per cent after six months.[146] Two years after the Ottawa enforcement effort, the rate had dropped back to 66 per cent, still, however, above the 58 per cent baseline.[147]

The most spectacular rise in the use of seat-belts in North America has been in Quebec, where use rates have risen from 53.4 per cent in 1985 to 67.7 per cent in 1986 and to 85.8 per cent in 1987. This has been accomplished through media publicity, police surveillance, and even token rewards.[148]

The wide variations in use in the United States, even among states with safety belt laws, can also be linked to the extent and methods of prosecution. One major consideration is whether the safety belt violation can be enforced alone, without linking it with another violation. Over two-thirds of states with compulsory use laws permit only secondary enforcement. Kansas, for example, requires that the person be ticketed for the primary offence before he or she can be cited for violation of the seat-belt law; in Pennsylvania, the person must actually be convicted of another offence.[149] Not surprisingly, belt usage is higher in primary enforcement states and lower where a secondary enforcement policy prevails.[150] Sixty-eight per cent of respondents who did not always buckle up said in a recent Michigan survey that they would increase their belt use if there were primary enforcement in Michigan.[151] Primary enforcement may account for the high rate of success in Elmira, which, as we saw, rose to almost 80 per cent in the spring of 1986 compared to a similar program in Modesta, California, where there is secondary enforcement only, which raised the use rate from 33 to 47 per cent.[152]

Another important factor, as discussed above, is the level of enforcement. A recent study at the University of North Carolina analysed use rates in relation to the level of enforcement and found, again, not surprisingly, that 'in both primary and secondary enforcement states, belt usage is higher in the presence of higher levels of enforcement.'[153] North Carolina, at the time of the study, had the highest US use rate, with 78 per cent front-seat occupants buckled up, three times the figure in September 1985, before the law became effective.[154] It would be instructive to study carefully why the rate is high in that state. No doubt the regime of primary enforcement is important. And, no doubt, the relatively high prosecution rate also plays a major role. Texas also has a high use rate, probably because it has primary enforcement, a fairly high fine, and a high rate of prosecution.[155] All these factors give a signal to drivers that the state means business. The success in North Carolina came after a year's enforcement when only warnings were given. Was this a factor in gaining acceptance because of the perceived fairness of giving time for adjustment?[156] Note that in Elmira, which is also successful, police had earlier used warning tickets: 2,000 warning tickets were given out over four days in April 1986.[157] Quebec has also made wide use of warning tickets.[158]

Publicity and education without increased enforcement have been found effective when concentrated on a specific plant. A nine-week seat-belt program conducted at a Transport Canada Centre in Cornwall, Ontario (using feedback signs and memos, and so on), raised use from 65 per cent to 82 per cent for drivers, and a similar program at a non-government Goodyear Canada plant in Collingwood, Ontario, increased seat-belt use from 33 per cent to 84 per cent.[159]

The point of having seat-belts is to reduce personal injuries. Is a safety belt effective in doing so? The answer is clearly yes. Persons who have buckled up are less seriously injured in accidents than persons in comparable situations who have not buckled up. This has been the conclusion of a large number of studies. A study of 28,000 accidents in Sweden reported in 1976 by Bohlin has been very influential in subsequent debates. Bohlin concluded that 'the safety belt offers "full" protection against fatal injury up to accident speeds of about 60 m.p.h.'[160] Mackay, an English expert, stated in 1981 that seat-belts could reduce the rate of fatalities by 50 or 60 per cent.[161] An OECD road safety research synthesis concluded that 'a safety belt, when properly used, will reduce serious injuries or fatalities by 40 to 50 per cent.'[162]

The most authoritative study of the effects of seat-belt legislation was the 1985 British government study, *The Medical Effects of Seat Belt Legislation in the United Kingdom.* The law, passed in 1982, was introduced for a three-year trial period only, and so an evaluation was done, comparing injury patterns for the year before and the year after implementation of the legislation.[163] Earlier studies from Australia had been commenced after legislation was in force and so did not contain comparisons with the state of affairs before the legislation.[164] Moreover, in the English study there were not the confounding problems of other significant changes in legislation at about the same time. This had happened in Ontario, where the safety belt laws were enforced the very month (February 1976) that speed limits were lowered, so it is not easy to say what can be attributed to speed reduction and what to safety belts.[165]

The English study stated: 'There is a unified view from investigators around the world that seat belts, while causing some relatively minor injuries, are an important means of protecting car occupants in crashes. The present study reaches a similar conclusion but it also fills a gap in the literature by presenting a comprehensive before and after study based on high quality medical data demonstrating the change in injury patterns associated with seat belt use legislation.'[166] In their study of fourteen British hospitals which admit 59 per cent of all patients with serious traffic injuries, the authors found a reduction of 20 per cent in severe injuries for drivers, 24 per cent in severe injuries for front-seat passengers, and 34 per cent in brain injuries.[167]

The concept of 'risk homeostasis,' discussed earlier, must be considered. Will the use of seat-belts actually increase the number of accidents, even if it helps those who wear them?

Much of the recent controversy surrounding this concept centres on seat-belts. The exchange between John Adams and Murray Mackay at the General Motors Symposium in 1984, 'Human Behaviour and Traffic Safety,' related mainly to seat-belts.[168] Adams, following Peltzman and Wilde, argues that 'protecting car occupants from the consequences of bad driving encourages bad driving.'[169]

A number of studies show that people wearing seat-belts do *not* drive less carefully than others. Evans et al. showed this to be so in examining freeways in Detroit and Ontario: in both a voluntary (Michigan at the time) and a mandatory scheme (Ontario) they found that belted drivers left longer headway between cars than non-users.[170] And Mackay, in England, showed no consistent relationship between belt wearing and speed.[171] But, of course, it is possible to argue that those who belt up may tend to be more cautious drivers than those who do not.

One US study comparing insurance claims for 1983–4 Cressidas, which have automatic belts, with claims for the comparable Nissan Maximas, which do not (so that the use rate would be relatively low), found a lower claim rate for cars with automatic belts. If the risk homeostasis theory is true, the regularly belted drivers would be involved in more accidents.[172] Of course, it is again possible to argue that cautious individuals may have chosen the car with the automatic belts.

A study by O'Neill, Lund, Zador, and Ashton examined driving behaviour before and after seat-belt legislation was introduced in Newfoundland and showed no increased risk-taking as compared to Nova Scotia, which had no legislation.[173] The 1986 OECD synthesis of research on seat-belt effectiveness in OECD nations concluded: 'The data indicate that large reductions in vehicle occupant deaths and injuries are possible and there is no evidence that these reductions are offset by increases in other areas, due to belted drivers taking more risks.'[174] No doubt Jonah and Lawson are correct in stating: 'Rather than trading off one risky behaviour for another, there is growing evidence that the same driver engages in a variety of risky behaviours such as speeding, impaired driving, following too closely and not wearing a seat belt.'[175] Perhaps if people can be encouraged to wear seat-belts, they might become more safety-conscious generally.[176]

It is not at all surprising that there is little if any compensation, let alone homeostasis, with seat-belt use. Drivers do not want to experience an accident, even if it is less severe than it might otherwise be. Moreover, safety features such as seat-belts provide little direct and immediate feedback to the driver and thus are distinguishable from other features, such as good brakes and faster car acceleration.[177]

The least cautious drivers, unfortunately, would seem to be the ones to belt up last.[178] Some studies have shown that young people are less likely to buckle up than older drivers.[179] The same is true for those who drive faster[180] and for those who drink and drive.[181] Thus, increasing the level of compliance should be increasingly effective as belt use levels increase. For this reason, the OECD study concludes, 'It is very important to pursue the steps necessary to reach the highest possible levels of safety belt use.'[182] Of course, achieving these levels becomes increasingly more costly in terms of enforcement personnel, extent of intrusions on privacy, penalties, and so on.[183]

Comparisons among jurisdictions and over time, noting changes in seat-belt use rates coupled with changes in the law, would help explain the effects of different compliance techniques. Why does use vary from city to city and from jurisdiction to jurisdiction? Why has seat-belt use, for example, been over 65 per cent in Houston and Dallas and only about 35 per cent in San Francisco and Los Angeles?[184] Both Texas and California have mandatory use laws. Is primary enforcement in Texas, but not in California, the reason? Is it the level of enforcement? The penalty?

One solution to the problem of seat-belt use is, of course, passive restraints, which do not depend on individual decisions. Airbags have the least chance of being disconnected by the owner and are extremely unlikely to be inadvertently deployed. Mercedes had, by the end of September 1987, 329,000 cars with airbags that had travelled 5 billion miles without a single inadvertent deployment.[185] Some automatic motorized non-detachable belts have achieved very high usage rates. Ninety-six per cent of drivers of Toyota Cressidas and Camrys with such belts were found to be using them, compared to 74 per cent with manual belts. There has been similar success with the Ford Escort and Mercury Lynx. However, Chrysler's detachable automatic belt had in 1987 produced poor results.[186] A 1988 US transportation department survey in US cities showed that 99 per cent of drivers with cars equipped with motorized shoulder belts were using them.[187] State Farm Insurance, the largest US vehicle insurance company, offers 10 per cent discounts for personal injury insurance for cars with automatic belts, 20 per cent for cars with driver airbags, and 40 per cent for cars equipped with both airbags and automatic belts.[188] Most major US automobile insurers now offer similar substantial discounts for automatic restraints, one company giving a 60 per cent discount for premiums for medical payments for occupants plus additional incentives for driver and front-seat passenger airbags.[189]

US Federal Motor Vehicle Safety Standard 208, enacted in 1984, required automakers to install automatic restraints, such as airbags and automatic belts, in 10 per cent of their 1987 model cars. They were required to put automatic restraints in 25 per cent of their 1988 models, 40 per cent in their 1989 models, and all of their 1990 models.[190] However, in order to encourage airbag development, which is considered more desirable than automatic seat-belts, the National Highway Traffic Safety Authority (NHTSA) has extended until September 1993 the period in which cars with a driver-side airbag and a manual seat-belt in the right-front-passenger seat can meet the federal safety standard for automatic restraints.[191] Safety standard 208 could have been rescinded if, by 1 April 1989, states accounting for two-thirds of the US population passed mandatory seat-belt use laws which complied with the requirements set by the government.[192] However, few if any states have passed laws that completely satisfy the standard.[193] So the standard is now in effect,[194] but subject to delay in implementation.

Sanctions and Speed Limits

The speed limit in Ontario, unless otherwise posted, is 100 km/h (i.e. about 62 mph) on major highways and 80 km/h (about 50 mph) on other highways. In cities it is 50 km/h, unless otherwise stated. Before 1976 the speed limits were 70 mph and 60 mph, having been raised from a maximum of 60 mph in 1968. These were reduced to 60 and 50 in 1976 and then with metrication in 1977 went up very slightly to the present limits. There were over 780,000 convictions for speeding in Ontario in 1986 – over two-thirds of all convictions under the Highway Traffic Act.[195]

The 55-mile-per-hour speed limit imposed by the US federal government in 1973, following the OPEC oil crisis, focused attention on the issue of speed. In order to conserve energy, Washington forced the states to enact 55-mph limits by the threat of withholding federal highway funds to states that did not comply. Designed as a temporary fuel-conservation measure, it became permanent because of the apparent safety benefits. Although public opinion initially generally supported the 55-mph limit, many drivers and many states, particularly in the west, did not. Some states reduced the penalty. Nevada, for example, reduced the penalty for speeding to a $5 fuel-wastage fine. Others provided that speeding should have no effect on insurance rates.[196]

The federal government put continuing pressure on the

states to enforce the law by requiring a stated degree of compliance. In 1986 the rule was that 50 per cent of traffic had to be at 55 mph or lower or else some highway funds would be withheld. Although most states did not achieve this objective, no state had funds withheld: the federal rules, through artificial devices such as speedometer error adjustments, allowed greater deviance without penalty.[197] Most recently, Congress passed legislation to permit states to increase the limit to 65 mph on rural expressways,[198] and then, by a margin of 67 to 33, narrowly exceeding the two-thirds majority needed (21 March 1987), the Senate overrode a presidential veto on the question.[199] As of April 1988, forty states had raised the speed on rural interstates to 65 mph.[200]

A driver travelling on any major road in Ontario at precisely the speed limit would find that he or she was being passed by most other drivers. One study in 1986 showed that 60 per cent of drivers in Ontario exceeded the speed limit.[201] This had been the pattern in the United States, where the majority of traffic exceeded the 55-mph limit, particularly on rural interstates, where almost three-quarters of drivers exceeded the limit in 1983.[202] Statistics from Quebec show that 85 per cent of vehicles travelling on one major autoroute in 1986 were travelling at 115 km/h or lower in a 100-km/h zone. Thus, at least 15 per cent of the traffic was above 115 km/h.[203]

How effective is the criminal process in controlling speed? A number of studies have tested the effect of a police cruiser at the side of the highway. Of course, it does have some effect, more so when the officer is engaged in detecting speeders than when he is occupied in actually writing a ticket.[204] Hauer and others have shown, however, that the effect of a police car will be dissipated a few miles away.[205] There is a 'distance halo' operating in both directions of the highway, and there is also a short-term 'time halo' operating for a few days after enforcement, and possibly also at the same time the following week, because people anticipate that the police may be there again.[206]

Some states have studied the effect of an increase of enforcement on a large segment of a highway system. California, for example, increased enforcement in 1982 on five heavily travelled interstates by allocating an additional $1.3 million for overtime enforcement. Compliance improved by 5 per cent – from 78.2 per cent who disobeyed the law to 74.7 per cent. Similar results were found in other studies. But when the patrol officers were removed, reductions in speed disappeared.[207]

Enforcing speeding laws uses a large amount of police resources and yet barely covers the highway system: in the United States it is estimated that there are 190 miles of highway for every on-duty patrol officer.[208] Increased enforcement is often concentrated on the better roads, the very roads that tend to be safer. This occurred after the federal government imposed the 55-mph speed limit. The requirement of a stated degree of compliance led states to set up radar patrols on major throughways, which constituted only 5 per cent of the roads but half the travel.[209] Oregon, for example, devoted one-third of its resources to monitoring freeway motoring, even though only 6 per cent of fatalities occurred there.[210]

Does increasing the speed limit increase accidents? We now appear to have a natural experiment. Will the death and accident toll on US interstate highways, freed from the 55-mph limit, now rise? No doubt it will, but because of increased speeds or of increased driving caused by more attractive speed limits? The studies we have seen do not adjust for exposure. The Insurance Institute for Highway Safety's headline in its *Status Report* of 26 December 1987 reads[211]: 'Caution: 65 MPH Speed is Hazardous to Your Life.' It shows that deaths rose by 52 per cent over a three-month period from May 1987 to July 1987 in the twenty-two states that had raised their limit. But it does not tell us how many more drivers there were on interstates than before and how many persons switched from less safe roads, where the speed was still 55 mph, to interstates. In fact, the evidence is consistent with greater safety: although deaths rose in the twenty-two states from 296 to 450 on the interstates, they dropped from 4,830 to 4,350 on other highways in those states. Overall, highway traffic deaths dropped in the states that had raised the speed limit. We will not know the true effect of raising the limit until more careful studies have been done, controlling for exposure.[212] Even if later studies show an increase in accidents per distance driven, this will not tell us whether the increase in mobility and time saved makes the trade-off justifiable.

When the 55-mph limit was first imposed, the accident rate decreased for 1974, to a considerable extent because of a decrease in exposure. There were higher prices and line-ups for gas, and it was thought to be unpatriotic to take unnecessary trips. When measured against the distance driven, however, the decrease in accidents and fatalities was still significant.[213] But – and this is the key question – would it have been the same without the 55-mph limit? Ontario did not decrease the speed limit until 1976, three years after the United States did. Ontario also showed a major decrease in fatalities in 1974[214] – even though the speed limit was still 70 mph.[215] In 1976 speed limits in Ontario were reduced from 70 to 60 mph and deaths showed a further major decrease, but it is difficult to separate speed reduction from the introduction of safety belts that year.[216] The fact that fatalities fell on all types of roads in 1976, even ones whose speed limits were not changed, indicates that speed may not have been the key consideration.[217]

The US National Research Council's study '55: A Decade of Experience', attributed much of the decline in highway fatalities following 1973 to reduced speed: 'The reduced speeds and reduced speed variance of 1974 appear to be key factors in the dramatic decline in highway fatalities in 1974. Nationwide statistics and more detailed analyses of state experience indicate that 3,000 to 5,000 lives were saved annually in the early years of the 55 mph speed limit. International experience with speed limits is consistent with this estimate.'[218]

In contrast, a 1986 study by the Brookings Institution on the regulation of automobile safety concluded that decreased speed may not have been the important variable, but rather automobile safety: 'Our estimates indicate that highway fatalities would be about 40 percent greater were it not for the safety features adopted since the beginning of this program.'[219] A time-series study found that 'the post-embargo years and their 55 mph speed limit do not seem to have a large effect upon total deaths,'[220] and a cross-sectional analysis found that 'SPEED [a statistical variable representing average highway speed] appears to contribute little to explaining the occupant death rate.'[221]

Reducing speed limits should, in theory, reduce the frequency and severity of accidents. The higher the speed, the slower the reaction time to a crisis, the longer it takes to stop, and the greater the impact and damage if there is a crash.[222] This analysis would seem to apply to city streets, but does it apply also to major rural highways? Low highway speeds, for example, may cause drivers to pay less attention to their task (an example of risk compensation?) and yet should, in fact, require greater concentration if other drivers habitually exceed the limit and thus cause more passing and variance than might occur if the speed limit were higher. Low highway speeds will also require more driving time, with the consequent greater possibility of fatigue and drowsiness.

Variance in speed is a very important consideration. The widely used US Department of Transportation handbook, *Synthesis of Safety Research, 1982*, states that 'the greater the variation in speeds on a given roadway, the higher the probability of an accident assuming equal exposure.'[223] The handbook examined a number of studies and concluded: 'The weight of evidence would lead to the conclusion that speed variance and accident frequency are directly related. The greater the absolute deviation from mean traffic speed the higher the accident rate.'[224]

Ezra Hauer explains the phenomenon in terms of changes of overtaking or passing characteristics. The greater the departure above or below the median speed, the greater the number of times a vehicle either is overtaken by or passes other vehicles, which, in turn, leads to increased accident risk.[225] The 1986 OECD synthesis of research agreed that 'accident risk increases with speed dispersion' but cautioned that the conclusion, 'while valid for homogeneous traffic, may not always be true if the proportion of heavy vehicles is significant.'[226] Variance in speed is an important subject which, as the National Research Council's Study 55 states, needs further study.[227]

In the past, traffic engineers set speed limits at the 85th percentile,[228] that is, the speed that 85 per cent of the drivers met on that roadway. As the Department of Transportation handbook states: 'This is the speed that 85 percent of the traffic is moving at or below and reflects the safe speed for the given roadway conditions as determined by a large majority of drivers. Solomon showed that the 85th percentile speed is in the speed range where the accident involvement rate is lowest. Other studies confirm this finding.'[229] Such an approach has the advantage of picking a speed that most people are comfortable with. This concept was recently advocated by a Quebec Task Force Report.[230]

Is there a danger in raising limits to current practice? It may be that drivers who are now exceeding the speed limit are kept alert in checking for police cars coming up behind them or stationed up ahead on the road. Will this alertness be lost if speed limits are raised? Moreover, will drivers now exceed the new limit, just as they exceeded the lower limit? Preliminary indications are that significant violations will still occur with a 65-mph limit. The first state to raise its speed limit to 65 mph on rural interstates was New Mexico, and nine weeks after the law was changed 49 per cent of cars were exceeding the limit, compared to 25 per cent who had exceeded 65 mph in 1986.[231] That rate had risen to 61 per cent of passenger cars by November 1987, with 21 per cent going over 70.[232] However, radar detectors are legal in New Mexico, as they are in all states except Connecticut, Virginia, and the District of Columbia.[233] The US Federal Highway Administration has rejected a proposed ban on radar detectors, saying that speed limit enforcement is a state, not a national, problem.[234] The relationship between radar detectors, speed, and accidents is largely unstudied. Detectors are banned in Ontario and four other provinces[235] but permitted in British Columbia: what effect does this have on safety?

Is there a relationship between speeding convictions and accidents? Mary Chipman studied the relationship between demerit points – following convictions for Ontario Highway Traffic Act offences – and accidents. She found a correlation, but in a later study, where she controlled for exposure (measured by distance driven in a week), the correlation disappeared except for drivers who drove only small distances.[236] This could well be true for speeding convictions. Those who travel more are more likely to get speeding citations; yet they may be less liable to have accidents than those who travel less when their increased exposure is taken into account. Moreover, the person who drives for a living and who may not be a serious risk on the road may tend to go faster than others. One study showed that drivers travelling over 100 miles drove on average 4 mph faster than others.[237] Speeding convictions operate, in effect, as a tax on their driving.

Reducing variance in speeds by raising the limit (to the 85th percentile) would seem to be worth careful consideration. Apart from the possibility of reducing accidents, it reduces the number of persons violating the law. Widespread disrespect of one law probably has some effect on citizens' respect for others.

Further, having a more realistic law reduces considerably the extremely wide discretion that the police have in enforcing the law. In the United States, when the 55-mph limit was in effect on all highways, there was wide variation in practice from one jurisdiction to another: about one-quarter of states allowed no tolerance, another quarter allowed people to go up to 5 mph above the limit, and a further quarter up to 10 mph (and some of these even higher), and a further quarter gave the officer full discretion.[238] Discretion is inherent whatever the limit is, but the more realistic the limit, the less the scope for discretion[239] – and therefore for its improper exercise.

To what extent is it desirable for the law to impose a uniform solution? Should the law, instead, adjust to different situations? Different limits on different highways or stretches of the same highway might bring about greater acceptance of the law. But will they create confusion? The 1986 OECD synthesis states: 'There is indirect evidence (research carried out in Finland) which suggests that speed limits matched to road characteristics may be more effective from the safety viewpoint than uniform limits on broad road categories.'[240] One concern about raising limits on selected roads is that there may be a carry-over or spill-over effect onto other, lower-speed roads. Studies have shown this to occur when drivers leave higher-speed highways, even when they come to a full stop before entering the lower-speed road.[241] The issue of broad versus specifically targeted laws is an important one which affects all fields of enforcement, not only traffic enforcement.

A further question: should there be a maximum *limit* or rather should there be a suggested *standard* for ideal conditions? The standard could be expressed to vary according to the road conditions. Or there might be a suggested range, say 80 to 120 km/h, depending on conditions. Or the accused could have a legal defence to a charge, as in California, if the speed was 'reasonable or prudent, having due regard for weather, visibility, the traffic,' and so on.[242] No doubt the police would find this more difficult to enforce and would probably oppose it. The present system is simple to operate and fits the needs of any quota system that exists in a department.[243] It encourages the use of police radar, however, which measures speed, not danger. Radar can determine whether the person is or is not breaking the speed limit. But it encourages the police to go after the easy cases in locations which are often the least dangerous and where people understandably increase their speed, sometimes referred to as 'fishing holes.'[244] It also encourages the police to catch people where there is not much traffic, so that the speeder can be easily isolated, and not to bother with dangerous speeders weaving from lane to lane in heavy traffic. Further, a speed limit causes drivers to think that they are entitled to drive at the speed limit, and some think even that those who drive below it should not be entitled to do so. Would it not be preferable to frame the law in terms of unreasonable speed in relation to prevailing conditions, including traffic flow? This would place more responsibility on drivers to regulate their own conduct. It would also cut down on the present excessive concentration on prosecutions for speeding.

Sanctions and Drunk Driving

Criminal sanctions are the main form of regulation directed at reducing traffic accidents involving drunk drivers.[245] Enormous resources are devoted to enforcement of criminal sanctions against drunk driving, through prosecutions and intensified enforcement campaigns designed to increase the certainty of apprehension. Canadian estimates suggest that as much as 30 to 40 per cent of court time is taken up with prosecutions of drunk driving offences, and American estimates suggest as many as 1.8 million drunk driving arrests in that country each year.[246] In recent years, increasing emphasis has been placed on the moral dimensions of the use of criminal sanctions against drunk driving, and governments and interest groups have consciously tried to 'criminalize' drunk driving, largely by increasing the severity of sanctions, so that it is not perceived as a commonplace, low-stigma 'folk crime,' in the manner of other traffic offences such as speeding.[247]

The structure of most criminal sanctions against drunk driving facilitates enforcement through requirements for mandatory supply of blood or breath samples and the use of an objective standard of liability based on scientific evidence of a driver's blood alcohol concentration (BAC).[248] Launched in Scandinavia in the 1930s and 1940s, in Britain and Canada in the late 1960s, and increasingly in the United States throughout the last two decades, such objective ('per se') sanctions have supplemented traditional criminal sanctions, which require specific proof of intoxication, alcohol impairment, or negligent driving behaviour in each case.

Per se laws depend on technological innovations such as reliable means to test BACs in samples of blood or breath and scientific evidence which determines the relation between increasing BACs and the risk of accidents. Although a few commentators have questioned the fairness of basing criminal liability on an objective standard, not readily determined by drivers, but justified by scientific evidence of the aggregate probability of danger when driving,[249] most have accepted objective per se laws and requirements for mandatory blood or breath testing as necessary for social protection. Courts in the United States and Canada have generally upheld per se sanctions, even though they do not require proof of guilty knowledge and contain mandatory or irrebuttable presumptions of guilt on proof of an elevated blood alcohol concentration.[250] As with speed limits, per se laws seem to have a tolerance zone in enforcement, with the average apprehended driver having a BAC level substantially above the minimum prohibited by law.[251] In both its requirement for mandatory self-incrimination and its objective standard of liability, the criminal sanction against drunk driving has been stretched about as far as it can go to facilitate easy enforcement. The question that remains is how effective this sanction has been in reducing traffic accidents.

After the introduction of widely publicized per se criminal sanctions in Britain in 1967 and Canada in 1969, reductions in alcohol-related fatal accidents were observed in both countries before they eventually returned to original and higher levels.[252] Within the framework of general deterrence theory, these reductions can be explained as a product of drivers' increased perceptions of their risk of punishment if they drove after drinking. They failed in the long run because the perception of risk eventually wore off, to reflect more realistic perceptions about the certainty of apprehension and punishment.[253] The introduction of per se laws in both countries did not increase the severity of punishment.[254] Per se laws may have increased the celerity of punishment by avoiding the need for proof of subjective judgments about behaviour in order to obtain a conviction.

Attempts to increase the severity of punishment are often met by significant distortion effects throughout the criminal justice system. Trial delays and not guilty pleas can more than double, as accused drivers seek to avoid or delay a more severe punishment.[255] Severe penalties, such as mandatory jail sentences, can also overburden prison capacities and do not seem to reduce recidivism.[256] Severe penalties may, however, have a general deterrent value, especially if combined with increased and well-publicized enforcement activity, and they may also help stigmatize drunk driving.[257]

The success of general deterrence strategies in reducing alcohol-related accidents is not a simple reflection of the number of arrests made. For example, more drunk driving

arrests were made in Canada than in Britain after imposition
of per se criminal sanctions, yet the British law was significantly more effective in reducing alcohol-related accidents
over a longer period.[258] Likewise, evaluations of the American Alcohol Safety Action Program and the British Columbia Counterattack program have suggested that the number
of drunk driving charges is not related to reductions in
alcohol-related accidents and that the arrest rates can be
doubled without necessarily reducing alcohol-related accidents.[259] The fact that increasing arrests alone does not seem
to deter drunk driving enough to reduce alcohol-related
accidents may in part reflect the low likelihood of apprehension (estimated by many to be as low as only one chance in
approximately every 500–2,000 impaired trips),[260] even
during peak enforcement activity.

Although, as the above evidence suggests, increasing
drunk driving arrests alone probably will not reduce alcohol-related accidents, some general deterrence campaigns
seem to reduce drunk driving and alcohol-related accidents.
The most effective campaigns seem to be those that not only
increase arrests but are well publicized through commercials
and news reports, target the high-risk night-time and weekend periods, and significantly raise perceptions of the likelihood of apprehension and punishment. The Cheshire blitz
in England, which was associated with significant reductions in serious traffic accidents during night-time 'drinking
hours,' was well publicized and involved a fifteenfold increase in administration of breath tests.[261] The Stockton
crackdown in California involved a seven- to tenfold increase in arrests on Friday and Saturday nights and produced an overall 15 per cent reduction in accidents during
that time of day. This reduction can probably be explained
by a corresponding reduction in the incidence of drunk
driving, as measured by the percentage of drivers randomly
tested in roadside surveys who were found to have been
drinking. Targeting high-risk periods appeared to be effec-

tive, as there was no apparent shift in accidents to other times or days of the week. The increased level of enforcement achieved during the Stockton crackdown was estimated to yield an apprehension rate of 1 in every 300 impaired trips.[262] Traffic safety effectiveness was greatest during periods in which the crackdown received intense publicity.

In general, publicity seems to be crucial in the general deterrence of drunk driving. One recent study even suggests that alcohol-related accidents in Arizona were reduced more through various forms of publicity that preceded the enactment of a stricter drunk driving law than through passage of the law itself.[263] In some cases publicity may be more important even than the structure of criminal sanctions or the actual level of enforcement activity, but in all cases it seems to be a necessary condition for successful deterrence of drunk driving in a manner that reduces alcohol-related accidents.[264]

Despite the above positive results, there are important limitations to the traffic safety effectiveness of campaigns to deter drunk driving. Most campaigns (except for the Stockton crackdown, which reduced accidents over the three and a half years of implementation) have been effective only in the short term, and some intensive enforcement campaigns have failed to produce observable traffic safety improvements. For example, increased enforcement in Toronto's Reduce Impaired Driving Everywhere (RIDE) program through the use of 'spot checks,' involving random stopping and questioning of drivers, did not seem to result in either less drunk driving, as measured by the percentage of randomly selected drivers with illegal BACs, or significant reductions in reported accidents.[265] The apparent lack of effectiveness may be related to three factors: not enough drivers were stopped to raise the perceived risk of apprehension, the program ran sixteen hours a day and did not target the high-risk night-time and weekend periods, and a very low number of drivers stopped were tested for alcohol.[266] For whatever reason, the RIDE program did not seem to increase people's perceptions that they would be apprehended if they drove after drinking during the period of its evaluation. The program continues to be implemented today, and it is not yet known if it has contributed to long-term attitudinal changes that may have helped reduce drunk driving.[267]

One enforcement technique that seems to increase perceptions of the likelihood of apprehension is extensive use of random breath testing. When such testing was introduced in the Australian state of New South Wales, approximately one million breath tests were administered to a driving population of three million during each of the first three years of its implementation. A catchy publicity slogan ('How will you go when you sit for the test? Will you be under 05 or under arrest?'), emphasizing both the certainty and severity of punishment, was used to good effect. Given this publicity and widespread testing, the program became well known among the population; in fact it became very likely that a breath test had been administered to almost all drivers or to their friends or family members. In this way, extensive random breath testing successfully increased the perceived likelihood of apprehension and punishment.

Recent evaluations of the program suggest that over the first three years of its implementation, fatal accidents involving alcohol were reduced on average 21 per cent each year, and fatal accidents between 11 p.m. and 3 a.m., a high-risk period for drunk driving, were reduced by over 40 per cent.[268] What is not known is whether the use of random breath testing or the fact that approximately one in every three drivers was stopped each year was primarily responsible for raising the perceived likelihood of apprehension enough to attain such impressive reductions in alcohol-related accidents. The existence of some offsetting effects cannot be ignored. For example, when random breath testing was conducted on the main roads of Adelaide, in South Australia, there was a significant migration of late-night

injury accidents to the back streets.[269] In support of the effectiveness of random breath testing as an enforcement technique, it must be noted that experimental evidence suggests
that police often fail to detect drinking among detained
drivers on the basis of visual clues alone.[270] Moreover, random breath testing in the state of Victoria also seemed to
yield impressive reductions in alcohol-related accidents
without stopping up to one in three drivers each year.[271]

Given the limited effectiveness of many but not all spot-
check programs, it is obvious that more research is needed
to understand how general deterrence campaigns can better
raise perceived likelihood of apprehension and punishment.
The preliminary evidence does, however, suggest that massive and well-publicized stopping of vehicles and perhaps
random breath testing may be necessary. Civil libertarians
are likely to object to the imposition of either of these measures, but from a traffic safety perspective their vocal objections should be welcomed: they will make the program
more newsworthy and in that way increase the deterrence of
drunk driving and the reduction of alcohol-related accidents. The random stopping of drivers has been criticized as
an intrusive and arbitrary means to investigate any
crime,[272] but courts have generally deferred to the state's
interests in using such methods to address the serious risks
created by drunk driving. The Supreme Court of Canada
has, for example, recently decided that random spot checks
arbitrarily detain drivers and deprive them of their right
upon detention to retain and instruct counsel without delay,
but it nevertheless held that the importance of highway
safety and the risk presented by drinking drivers justified
such limits on constitutional rights.[273]

Another intervention that could increase certainty of
apprehension is the use of temporary road-side licence
suspensions. In several Canadian and American jurisdictions, licences can be temporarily suspended for a short
period when drivers are apprehended with positive BACs.

The availability of suspensions for drivers not necessarily over the limit prescribed in the per se sanctions increases the range of targeted drivers and signals movement toward a compliance-based as opposed to a prosecution-based approach. The deterrent value of the temporary suspension is, however, questionable because of its relative leniency. Drivers are only temporarily deprived of the use of their vehicles, and they may have to pay towing costs. The value of the increased celerity of this sanction does not seem to compensate for its leniency.[274]

Proposals to increase the severity of temporary suspensions while also increasing certainty of apprehension have some merit,[275] but there are constitutional and practical limits to the severity of any sanction that is imposed summarily by administrative means. As with random breath testing, distinctions between this sanction's effectiveness in general and specific deterrence must be drawn. Stopping and testing more drivers may raise perceptions of the likelihood of apprehension and punishment among the general population of drivers; they are not, however, likely to apprehend and incapacitate greater proportions of those drivers with very high BACs, who present the greatest risk of having serious traffic accidents.[276] Such high-risk drivers can probably be better identified and apprehended by more traditional patrol methods, based on observation of erratic driving.

In addition to their role in raising the certainty and severity of punishment, criminal sanctions are increasingly used in order to stigmatize drunk drivers and create moral inhibitions against drunk driving. As we shall see, however, it remains an open question whether and how recently observed reductions in alcohol-related fatalities are related to changes in attitudes toward drunk driving.

Although the consensus of research suggests that the general deterrence of drinking and driving is difficult to achieve and sustain, recent research has cautioned that it may be unrealistic to expect simple and quick results from the use of criminal sanctions designed to increase severity and certainty of punishment. For example, when H.L. Ross examined the historical rates of alcohol-related accidents in Scandinavian countries using interrupted time-series analysis (suited for evaluating interventions 'expected to have a sharp, sudden impact'),[277] he found no 'scientifically acceptable evidence'[278] to support the hypothesis that passage of the famous Scandinavian per se laws reduced alcohol-related traffic accidents. Nevertheless, Ross admitted that lower rates of alcohol-related accidents in Scandinavia could be explained by diverse socio-cultural factors, such as attitudes toward drinking, availability and pricing of alcohol, and the strength of temperance-oriented pressure groups.[279]

Much of the recent study has tried more systematically to evaluate socio-cultural factors that may influence drinking and driving behaviour.[280] An understanding of socio-cultural, situational, and moral constraints is needed because as in other fields, such as compliance with the income tax laws, the 'rational person' is most probably not presented with sufficient threats of punishment to explain the amount of compliance and socially desirable behaviour that is actually achieved.[281] One study has estimated that based on the average fine of $335 received for a drinking and driving offence in New Brunswick and based on a robust apprehension rate of 1 in every 200 impaired trips, the ex ante cost of an impaired trip to a driver is only $1.70.[282] Of course, given the current use of more severe sanctions, including jail sentences and licence suspensions, the costs are often likely to be higher, although still discounted by very low rates of apprehension. Given the ease and comfort that the use of an automobile provides after drinking, an appropriate question for research seems to be why do more people not drive after drinking?

Some evidence is beginning to accumulate that suggests that in recent years a complex set of socio-cultural factors –

as diverse as new concerns about health and corresponding willingness to use law as a 'paternalistic instrument'[283] and intervention by victim pressure groups such as MADD[284] – have helped produce a moral and social climate in which drinking and driving may be less acceptable. Johannes Andenaes was perhaps the first theorist to suggest that development of moral inhibition and habits would have greater and more permanent value in preventing drinking and driving than creation of exaggerated fears of punishment through enforcement campaigns.[285]

Criminal sanctions can play a role, not only as an instrument to control behaviour through the imposition of threats of punishment, but as both a reflection of and an influence on society's culture and morals. At the same time, however, some scepticism must be retained, as the socio-cultural factors that would reduce drunk driving are difficult to understand or evaluate, let alone consciously manipulate. Moreover, socio-cultural, habitual, or moralistic approaches may not as readily affect those who have severe problems with alcohol or who are members of a deviant subculture.[286]

A variant of the socio-cultural approach is one that stresses that drinking and driving are complex types of behaviour dependent on the interaction of individual and environmental factors. Such an interactionist perspective suggests that sanctions should not only be used to create disincentives for individuals who 'decide'[287] to combine drinking and driving but should also be directed at 'gatekeepers,'[288] such as commercial vendors, social hosts, friends, and parents, who control environmental factors that contribute to drinking and driving. More generally, the range of enforcement actors should expand beyond state actors in the criminal justice system to include the use of moral inhibitions on the part of potential drunk drivers and interventions by private parties to stop their friends from driving after drinking. If such a social process is indeed taking place, we would expect people to change habits and develop moral inhibitions against drinking and driving and for private parties to intervene more frequently to stop drunk driving.[289] Yet very little research has been directed toward understanding these complex sociological processes.

Much effort has been devoted to prevention of drunk driving recidivism, but the various specific deterrence strategies used have demonstrated, at best, limited effectiveness.[290] The emphasis placed on the specific deterrence of convicted drunk drivers is demonstrated by the fact that most criminal sanctions have traditionally been structured to increase the severity of punishment for recidivists. The strong cultural image of the recidivist 'killer drunk'[291] who must be punished more severely belies the fact that most studies suggest that only approximately 15 per cent of those drunk drivers involved in fatal accidents have prior convictions for drunk driving.[292] The specific deterrence of convicted drunk drivers has often occupied attention and resources disproportionate to its traffic-safety importance.

In terms of reducing subsequent accidents, the most effective specific deterrent strategy has been use of long-term licence suspensions, although it is not known what combination of increased care levels and reduced activity levels account for the reduced accident rates of suspended drivers.[293] Evaluations of mandatory jail sentences have not suggested that such severe sanctions significantly reduce recidivism.[294] Some forms of expensive long-term educative or rehabilitative treatment have been shown effective in reducing recidivism, but in general evaluations of such specific deterrence strategies have not yielded impressive traffic safety results.[295]

In short, general deterrence strategies appear to be able to reduce alcohol-related accidents over the short term if they raise subjective perceptions about likelihood of apprehension. Eventually these perceptions seem to erode to reflect the reality of continued low likelihood of apprehension. Increasing either number of arrests or severity of sanctions alone, without publicity aimed at increasing perceived likelihood of apprehension, does not appear to reduce traffic accidents. The most successful general deterrence strategies appear to be those that increase the threat of apprehension through publicity and through perhaps some combination of stopping massive numbers of drivers or use of random breath testing. In general, however, it appears difficult to raise the certainty of apprehension and/or severity of punishment to the levels required to deter drunk driving enough to reduce alcohol-related traffic accidents without placing significant strains on the enforcement and conviction capacities of the criminal justice system or provoking concerns about excessive restrictions on mobility and privacy.

Even if enforcement of criminal sanctions does not often result in impressive or lasting reductions in traffic accidents, its educative and moralizing features may be contributing to a process of socio-cultural change, in which most people will, through a complex of habit, moral values, peer pressure, and other socio-cultural factors, not drive after consuming dangerous amounts of alcohol. A body of research is only just beginning to be developed to explore how drunk driving sanctions contribute to the socio-cultural climate and how that climate affects the incidence of drinking and driving behaviour. At this time, however, it cannot be claimed with confidence that sanctions can change the socio-cultural climate in a way that will stop people from driving after drinking to the extent needed to reduce alcohol-related accidents significantly.

Many of the themes that run through the entire traffic safety field also characterize our understanding of the control of drunk driving. Too much reliance has probably been placed on enforcement of sanctions by the police and obtaining of convictions in courts. Arrest and prosecutions should be used strategically and selectively in order to obtain optimal reductions in traffic accidents. The well-publicized drunk driving crackdown targeting high-risk periods is almost certainly more effective in reducing traffic accidents than the haphazardly located and concealed 'speed trap,' largely because sanctions in the latter intervention are not used selectively or strategically. Even when enforcement is intensified and carefully planned, however, the low probability of apprehension limits the effectiveness of police enforcement of criminal sanctions in reducing drunk driving.

Too much emphasis has been placed also on specific deterrent strategies, whether they be the concern with the recidivist demonstrated in the structure of the criminal law, which increases penalties for subsequent convictions, or use of expensive jail sentences or rehabilitative treatments for convicted drunk drivers, even though such interventions have not yielded impressive traffic safety results. The most effective form of specific deterrence for the drunk driver is licence suspensions, which operate primarily by reducing driving activity but may also increase the care taken when suspended offenders continue to drive. In any event, specific deterrent strategies target only a small proportion of the drunk drivers who will have serious traffic accidents in the future.

A few comments about our thoughts on how best to attack the drunk driving problem may help put the role of sanctions in a broader perspective. As throughout the traffic safety field, we are most optimistic about strategies that are based on compliance as opposed to deterrence models of social control and that reduce exposure to drinking and/or driving. As will be discussed below, raising the minimum drinking age seems to reduce alcohol-related accidents among the affected age groups, and the potential of addressing the drunk driving problem through pricing and taxing of alcohol remains 'untapped.' Drunk driving countermeasures should not be solely a matter of proactive policing in the pursuit of deterrence through obtaining convictions but should, through use of less punitive compliance tech-

niques, enlist the aid of commercial and social servers of alcohol, parents, and employers in preventing drinking and
driving. The regulatory techniques of civil liability, insurance pricing, and licensing will play a greater role in
implementation of both exposure-reducing and compliance
strategies. The optimal approach to reduce drunk driving
will be a comprehensive one that strategically makes use of
sanctions, environmental regulation, and limitations on the
availability of alcohol. We suggest that any drunk driving
program be designed with an awareness that drunk driving
can be understood as a transportation, alcohol, driving, or
socio-cultural problem.

One last caveat: regulation of drunk driving is the regulation of a form of driving behaviour and, as such, subject to
the limitations encountered in the regulation of all forms of
driving behaviour. Most policy discussions of drunk driving
portray an unrealistic message that alcohol is the sole causal
factor in all traffic accidents which involve a drinking driver.
Of course, drivers with high BACs are at much greater risk of
having a traffic accident, and drunk driving is a factor in a
large proportion of serious accidents; but 'alcohol is neither
a necessary nor sufficient condition for collision occurrence.
It is not a necessary condition because many collisions occur
in which alcohol was not involved; it is not a sufficient
condition because the vast majority of drinking drivers
never crash.'[296]

Focus on alcohol as the prime casual factor in large numbers of serious accidents has often blinded both research and
policy communities to the epidemiological insight that
prevention of the prime 'cause' of accidents is not always
the most effective means to prevent accidents or reduce the
damage sustained.[297] Driving behaviour, even risky and
unacceptable behaviour such as drunk driving, is not as
substantial a determinant of automobile accidents as is
commonly assumed. One regression analysis underlines this
insight by suggesting that while the successful introduction

of per se drunk driving sanctions in Britain accounted for 2.7 per cent of the variance in traffic casualties, distance driven and rainfall account for 48.8 per cent of the variance.[298]

A drastic shift of resources to an environment-centred approach, in which drunk driving is treated as a given form of driver behaviour, is not warranted, given the successes observed and documented in deterring drunk driving and reducing alcohol-related accidents. Nevertheless, various forms of roadway and vehicle design features, to be discussed in greater detail below, seem to have greater potential in reducing both frequency and severity of alcohol-related traffic accidents than is usually recognized. For example, road design features such as raised rumble strips or median lines may help prevent accidents, as they can counter the depressive effects of alcohol on the senses of drivers. One California study suggests that placement of large 'wrong-way – go-back' signs on both sides of off ramps facing wrong-way drivers can be very effective in reducing wrong-way crashes, the majority of which are alcohol-related.[299] Automobile design features that lessen the severity of injuries will, of course, reduce the damage sustained in alcohol-related accidents, especially because those impaired by alcohol seem more susceptible to trauma.[300] Breath test or performance interlocks can now be added to vehicles, either to prevent driving or to trigger an automobile's lights and horn as a warning if a car is driven after the driver has failed a preliminary breath or performance test.[301] The costs and political hazards of mandating any design features that reduce mobility are formidable,[302] but such interventions can reduce exposure of drunk drivers and their victims to harm without relying on the difficult task of preventing the combination of drinking and driving.

The above examples of effective forms of environmental design are only speculations based on the sparse research available, and they should not be taken as a suggestion to abandon use of sanctions against drunk driving. Selective

use of sanctions can help to prevent alcohol-related accidents, but real limits exist on how much the certainty and
severity of punishment can be raised. Sanctions may also
contribute to socio-cultural change, but more research is
needed to discover if the moralizing and educative effects of
sanctions can lead to changes in drinking and driving behaviour that will significantly reduce alcohol-related accidents.

2
Civil Liability, Insurance, and Deterrence

One of the longest-standing legal sources of discouragement of driver error or wrong-doing is the threat of a tort action by an injured victim against the driver whose negligence caused the injury. Such actions remain available today to auto accident victims and are widely used, despite the emergence over time of many other traffic accident counter-measures, including public sanctions directed at delinquent drivers. In a tort action, if successful, the wrong-doer in theory stands liable for all losses sustained by the victim in the form of foregone future income, medical costs, and pain and suffering. In the event of the victim being killed in the accident, the wrong-doer stands liable for economic losses sustained by dependants, as well as more recently in Ontario for loss of 'guidance, care, and companionship' sustained by both dependent and non-dependent relatives.[303]

In an economic framework of analysis, the threat of civil liability for these losses is assumed to operate much as the threat of a fine does on the behaviour of a prospective wrong-doer. It is assumed that the latter, in choosing a course of conduct, will weigh the expected costs of an accident (the losses for which he or she will be liable if it occurs, multiplied by the probability of it occurring if such a course

of conduct is chosen) against the costs of adopting some
alternative course of conduct that will avoid, or reduce the
probability of, the accident (i.e. accident costs will be
weighed against avoidance costs).[304] If the latter costs are less
than the former, rational drivers, confronting this calculus,
will avoid the conduct that may lead to an accident and if
they fail to do so will be found liable in negligence in a
subsequent tort action by the victim. This version of the
negligence concept involves, of course, a form of cost-benefit
calculus both by the driver and by a court in any subsequent
tort action. In theory, a legal regime embodying this calculus
should lead to socially efficient forms of driver behaviour on
the highways (although not necessarily efficient activity
levels, given that the higher incidence of accidents associated with higher activity levels is not considered in the
conventional negligence test).

However, while minimizing the sum of accident and
avoidance costs is efficient, the risk of confronting a large
liability judgment entails costs. On the usual assumption
that most individuals are risk averse, risk is a source of
disutility, and such individuals will be prepared to pay a
fixed or certain sum in excess of the expected costs of the
risk in order to shift some or all of the risk of driver-error to
another. To the extent that other parties exist who are less
risk averse, a welfare-enhancing exchange is possible. This is
the role of insurance. Insurers, by pooling large numbers of
similar but uncorrelated risks, are able to diversify away the
individual risks in the pool and estimate a near-certain loss
experience over the pool over any given period of time. In
return for a loading fee (reflecting administrative costs) and
a return on capital, insurers will be prepared to bear risks at
a cost that is less than the cost that these risks represent to
the individuals who would otherwise bear them.

Just as accident and avoidance costs are real social costs,
so too are the costs (or disutility) associated with risk bearing. If these costs can be reduced by shifting them from

more to less risk-averse parties, social welfare has been enhanced.[305] However, these two forms of efficiency (efficient accident reduction and efficient risk reduction) entail unavoidable trade-offs. To the extent that insurance is not possible or available (liability insurance was historically considered contrary to public policy), the deterrent effects of the civil liability system will be maximized by fully internalizing accident cost to wrong-doers, but the costs (or disutility) associated with risk bearing will also be maximized. To the extent that complete insurance is available, the costs of risk bearing will be eliminated, but so too will the costs of causing accidents, which will have been partly externalized (at a price) onto others (insurers).

Thus, coexistence of civil liability and third- and first-party liability insurance, or particular combinations of the two, substantially complicates analysis of the deterrent effects of the tort system on driving behaviour.[306] Third-party insurance provides coverage to the insured against liability to third parties for losses caused by the insured's legally culpable conduct. First-party insurance provides coverage to the insured against his or her own accident losses, however caused. Both kinds of insurance affect the deterrent properties of the tort system as it relates to auto accidents. In almost all jurisdictions, coexistence of tort law and insurance is institutionalized through compulsory auto insurance requirements, either through third-party regimes, designed principally to ensure that victims of the negligence of others are not confronted with a judgment-proof defendant,[307] or through first-party regimes, to ensure that injured parties do not lack access to resources.

A pure third-party tort-insurance regime influences motorists to take care toward others, by third-party liability insurance premiums, deductibles, and uninsured excess liability, and to take self-protective measures, by the fact that these losses are uninsured. A pure first-party regime that does not recognize third-party claims (i.e. first-party no-

fault) gives motorists no direct incentives to take care
toward third parties but gives them incentives to take self-
protective measures, in part because of implications for first-
party insurance premiums and in part because under most
typical first-party systems all pecuniary and non-pecuniary
losses are not fully compensated. What is the empirical
evidence on the safety implications of moving from a fault-
based–third-party insurance regime to various forms of no-
fault–first-party insurance regimes?[308]

Landes[309] examined data from fifteen US states that had
adopted partial no-fault schemes and found that fatalities in
each state had increased by between 376 and 1,009 a year.
All US no-fault schemes preserve the right to sue in some
contexts. Add-on no-fault schemes (like that in Ontario)
permit suit in all cases but require subtraction of no-fault
benefits from awards against third parties. Threshold no-
fault regimes prohibit suit under stipulated thresholds but
permit suits above them. Such thresholds vary widely. They
are typically either monetary or verbal. In the case of monetary thresholds, medical expenses incurred by an accident
victim beyond a specified dollar threshold trigger the right
to sue. In the case of verbal thresholds, injuries that entail,
for example, 'serious and permanent physical impairment'
trigger such a right.

Landes claims, on the basis of her data, that a monetary
threshold of as low as $1,500 is likely to result in a 10 per
cent increase in fatalities.[310] Most commentators find the
conclusion quite implausible, given the relatively modest
no-fault elements of the insurance mix in many states, in
particular the preservation of the right to sue for most
serious injuries, and have been critical of aspects of her
empirical method.[311] In addition, private first-party
insurance schemes retain significant risk-rating characteristics that are likely to discourage many of the same forms of
driving behaviour that are discouraged by risk-rating under
third-party insurance. Three subsequent studies of US data

find no significant effects on fatality rates from adoption of no-fault regimes,[312] although a fourth study finds that no-fault states have experienced increases in loss ratios of between 3.9 per cent and 7.4 per cent, depending on the extent of no-fault features.[313]

Brown examined auto fatality rates in New Zealand following adoption of a universal accident compensation scheme in 1972 (which effectively abolished all tort claims for personal injuries) and found that the rate continued to decrease after adoption. However, he acknowledges that other safety factors may also have been influential during this period – mandatory seat-belt usage laws, crackdowns on drunk driving, speed-limit reductions – so that in the absence of a multivariate analysis (which he does not undertake) his findings are of very limited value.[314] However, McEwin, in undertaking such an analysis of the effects of the adoption of no-fault regimes in Australia and New Zealand, finds that in those jurisdictions that completely abolished tort claims and adopted non-risk-rated first-party premium structures (such as New Zealand), road fatalities have increased by 16 per cent per capita.[315]

Gaudry conducted a very detailed multivariate analysis of accident and fatality rates in Quebec before and after adoption of a pure no-fault automobile insurance scheme in 1978. The Quebec scheme, which is administered by an agency of the provincial government, bars all third-party personal injury claims arising out of auto accidents, provides for a high level of earnings-related benefits up to an income ceiling, and provides for financing of the scheme by flat levies on all motorists. Gaudry found that bodily injury accidents increased by 26.3 per cent a year following adoption and fatalities by 6.8 per cent (equivalent to 100 additional deaths a year).[316] While the increase in accident rates may reflect partly reporting bias, the fatality rate is not subject to this problem, and Gaudry's findings in this respect have attracted widespread attention.

Gaudry is inclined to attribute the increase in accident and fatality rates in part to the more stringent enforcement of compulsory insurance requirements, causing previously uninsured motorists now to drive less carefully, and partly to adoption of a flat-premium pricing regime that drastically reduces the cost of automobile insurance for high-risk drivers (e.g. young males), thus encouraging them to drive, when previously they were priced off the Quebec highways. The assumption here appears to be that young male drivers, for example, are risk preferrers and will be more influenced in their behaviour by a certainty of present costs, namely, substantial insurance premiums, than a mere probability of a substantial penalty for misconduct, even if the penalty entails the same expected costs as the insurance premium. Alternatively, young drivers, because of fewer resources than other drivers on average, have more price elastic demands for driving (including compulsory insurance) and are disproportionately influenced by changes in prices.

Devlin, in a recent detailed analysis of the Quebec experience,[317] reaches even more striking conclusions. She finds that adoption of the no-fault regime led to more high-risk and fewer lower-risk drivers on Quebec highways, accounting for a small increase (1 or 2 per cent) in fatalities, but more important, that average care levels fell substantially after introduction of no-fault, causing a 9.6 per cent increase in fatal accidents (or 154 more deaths a year). She concludes 'that a liability system for automobile accidents which operates in the presence of liability insurance still provides incentives for more prudent driving than does a no-fault system with insurance. Furthermore, the tying of insurance premiums to driving behaviour is essential if one wants individuals to exercise more care when driving.'[318]

In the light of the above studies, what assessment is possible of the effects of tort-insurance regimes on incentives for accident reduction? One view is that tort liability, even standing alone, will probably have few major incentive effects, and none once third-party insurance is introduced, so that movement to a first-party no-fault system is unlikely to reduce safety. This view turns largely on perceptions of the nature of errors involved in most automobile accidents. A 1970 study by the US Department of Transportation[319] concluded that 'the vast majority of accidents involve that large group of drivers with low accident likelihoods – drivers who, over their lifetime, will be involved in no more than a handful of state reportable accidents.' The study found that it is a fallacious view that the 'drivers who "cause" accidents are ... a small identifiable group that is guilty of hazardous driving, vastly over represented in accident statistics, and responsible for the "accident problem" ... Most drivers are often "guilty" of driver error. A certain magnitude of driver error is representative of the behaviour of the general average of drivers, and must be considered as normal, even though such behaviour departs from "standard", "correct", or "ideal" behaviour.'[320] One study estimates that a driver makes 200 observations per mile, 20 decisions per mile, and one error every two miles. Those errors result in a near-collision once every 500 miles, a collision once every 61,000 miles, a personal injury to some individual once every 530,000 miles, and a fatal accident once every 16 million miles.[321]

However, this view proves too much. If it is asserted in its extreme form, not only civil sanctions but criminal and administrative sanctions are all likely to prove futile. Driver error is an inherent manifestation of human fallibility. A similar argument is sometimes made that conduct on the highway that is dangerous to others is also typically dangerous to oneself, and no one wants to injure himself or herself. Thus, civil and presumably other sanctions add nothing to this desire for self-preservation. Again, this argument, if true, makes all sanction regimes for driving conduct futile. But some drivers are in fact likely to be less diligent in assessing risks than others; some drivers may have a stronger taste for risks than others. In these cases, sanctions, including civil sanctions that raise the cost of risk-taking, may affect behaviour. The appropriate question is whether, at the margin, some driver errors will be reduced by civil and other sanctions. While the presence of third- or first-party insurance will mute the incentive effects of civil liability in various ways, focus must be redirected to what risks are insured, what risks are uninsured, and, in particular, how the insurance is priced.

To the extent that accident rates are a function of activity or exposure levels (i.e. miles driven), as several empirical studies find,[322] then to the extent that insurance premium levels geared to exposure levels reduce activity levels, accident rates are likely to fall. In this respect, premiums would ideally be geared to distance driven and the driving conditions in which those distances are driven (urban, rural, business or leisure). Territorial classifications and business-leisure driving distinctions are able to capture (albeit crudely) some of the qualitative aspects of exposure levels, but distance driven is difficult and expensive to predict and monitor and is typically not employed as a primary rating variable. However, age and sex as rating variables also function as crude proxies for both quantitative and qualitative aspects of exposure levels, namely, young men as a class drive more distance and engage in more seriously risky behaviour than young women, and both groups are over-represented in accident statistics relative to the adult population at large.[323]

Gaudry's study of Quebec's no-fault system suggests that reducing the driving activity levels of high-risk driver classes is an important function of insurance pricing (in practice, by in effect forcing a binary choice between driving unlimited amounts or not driving at all, given that the distance driven by members of high-risk driving classes cannot be closely monitored and priced). Thus, proposals to abolish age and sex as automobile insurance rating variables for either third- or first-party insurance seem seriously misconceived from a safety perspective.

In Ontario, recently enacted legislation establishes a rate-review board to regulate premiums for third-party private automobile insurance and prohibits the use of age and sex as rating variables.[324] This prohibition will substantially reduce insurance premiums for young male drivers and will increase premiums for most other insured motorists. The resulting rate structures are directly antithetical to promotion of greater traffic safety: as earlier noted, young male drivers are heavily over-represented in traffic accident statistics. However, from an ethical perspective, it will be argued that rating categories that turn on age or sex are over-inclusive and penalize, or discriminate against, low-risk individuals within these categories on account of non-controllable ascriptive characteristics.

To the extent that accident rates are a function not only of activity levels but also of care levels, then, as Devlin's study of Quebec's no-fault system finds, absence of significant deductibles and failure to price insurance so as to reflect differential risks that individual drivers present to others (third-party insurance) or themselves (first-party insurance) are likely significantly to reduce care levels. Thus, under a first-party no-fault system, failure to differentiate premiums by reference to previous accident experience or previous traffic violations or demerit points is likely significantly to increase accident rates, even though such differentiation entails de facto importation of notions of fault or accident propensity into the setting of no-fault premiums, albeit not the right to claim compensation.[325]

However, this importation will inevitably lead to due process concerns – demands for arbitration and appeal procedures – over rate classification or increase decisions. By definition, these will be cruder under any risk-classification system than highly individuated tortious determinations of fault. Even with extensive risk-rating of premiums under a no-fault ('no-blame') first-party insurance scheme, safety incentives might be attenuated relative to tort–third-party insurance regimes, where tort law still operates to stigmatize certain kinds of conduct and arguably helps to reinforce socially responsible attitudes to risk-taking.[326] The Ontario government has recently announced that it is committed to introducing some form of auto no-fault regime, and the Ontario Automobile Insurance Board is currently (April 1989) conducting public hearings on several no-fault options.[326a]

This section has confined its focus to the impact of civil liability–insurance regimes on driver behaviour. However, while not pursued in this study, such regimes may affect other aspects of the traffic safety complex. For example, tort claims may be possible against manufacturers of defective or uncrashworthy motor vehicles or accessories (e.g. motorcycle helmets);[327] against negligent highway design, maintenance, and clean-up agencies;[328] against commercial servers or social hosts who allow patrons and guests who have consumed excessive amounts of alcohol to drive their cars;[329] against municipalities for failures of omission or commission by police or emergency services; and against doctors and hospitals for inadequate post-accident treatment.[330]

All these contexts raise difficult issues as to the likely impact of civil liability insurance regimes on frequency and severity of traffic accidents. By way of illustration, an important limitation on the impact of commercial server liability and regulation is that only approximately 25 per cent of those drivers involved in alcohol-related accidents consume their alcohol in commercial establishments.[331] Furthermore, the liability standard for serving an obviously intoxicated person is said by some commentators not to include many drivers who are sufficiently impaired to present a high accident risk.[332] However, servers and social hosts may become efficient cost avoiders when potential drivers become so intoxicated, and they may be in the optimal position to stop their guests from driving after excessive drinking.[333] The imposition of social host liability has, however, been politically unpopular and resisted by legislatures, and the deterrent effects of awards could be muted by the effects of insurance.[334]

3
Rewards

Anglo-American law has historically favoured punishment over rewards.[335] No doubt most English monarchs agreed with Machiavelli that 'it is much safer to be feared than loved, if one of the two has to be wanting.'[336] Bentham also took the view that if one had to choose one or the other, it is better to choose punishments than rewards. 'By punishment alone,' he wrote, 'it seems not impossible but that the whole business of government might be carried on.'[337] Note, however, that he added: 'Though certainly not so well carried on as by a mixture of that and reward together.'[338] In general, the liberal state has controlled the conduct of its citizens through the threat and imposition of sanctions as opposed to the offering of rewards to obtain compliance with desired forms of behaviour.

One major problem with rewards in earlier periods was that the state had limited wealth to pay for them.[339] Rewards were, however, used in non-monetary areas such as patents, copyright and salvage, and, of course, creation of honours. The payment of informers was one of the rare areas where money was actually paid out. Today, however, the state has tremendous wealth. As Charles Reich stated in a major article in 1964: 'Government is a gigantic syphon. It draws in revenue and power, and pours forth wealth: money, benefits, services, contracts, franchises and licenses.'[340]

One area where the state used rewards in the nineteenth century was in administration of prisons.[341] Persons within prisons were – and still are – rewarded for good behaviour by getting special privileges and 'time off.' The penal system that relied so heavily on punishments turned to rewards along with punishment once a person was incarcerated.

Like the prison authorities, many institutions have found that rewards can achieve objectives better than sanctions. Religious institutions have used grand incentives such as heaven and reincarnation.[342] The professorial world operates almost entirely through rewards (promotion, merit increases, prizes, and so on) rather than penalties. Businesses often use rewards to encourage workers to perform well in such areas as productivity, occupational safety, and sales performance.[343] Further, senior managers usually receive a significant proportion of their remuneration from incentives, dividends, and share price increases; one leading firm of consultants recommends that at least half the remuneration should come from these sources.[344] The us federal government has recently been providing productivity bonuses for its senior managers.[345] The Soviet Union is reported now to be applying productivity standards to employees at all levels, eventually affecting 75 million workers.[346]

To achieve objectives, government increasingly offers its citizens carrots such as tax deductions or credits, rebates, or grants and subsidies in such areas as encouraging insulation, planting trees, protecting the environment,[347] and scientific research.[348] Costs are not easy to control, however. Once an incentive program has been announced and is under way, it cannot fairly be cut off to the detriment of people who have completed conduct undertaken on the strength of the incentive – that is, without being accused of retroactivity. Governments have been increasingly using monetary rewards to encourage desirable conduct by criminal justice administrators: to the police to decrease the crime rate; to localities to use probation rather than jail; and to district attorneys in New York City to cut down on long-term detainees awaiting trial.[349]

Incentives tend to be used to get people to act – often a defined, manageable group. It is more difficult to use incentives to prevent action (not stealing, for example) because everyone fits into that category except those who do the act.[350] Although some have expressed the view that 'the law cannot reward a few in order to encourage the many,'[351] in theory there is no reason why an exemplary reward (for example, selecting by lot one person to be grandly rewarded) cannot be given.

As we move closer to a compliance-based model of enforcement, there will be greater emphasis on rewards. This is because, as Albert Reiss has pointed out, 'Where penalty systems primarily manipulate punishments, compliance systems principally manipulate rewards.' This is as true in traffic as in other fields.[352]

One area where firms have been successful in using rewards is in safety,[353] including traffic safety. Experience rating in workers' compensation schemes can be viewed as a reward as well as a sanction. The rebates and surcharges involved apply directly to the firm, not specifically to employees. Let us examine schemes that apply to employees directly.

The Toronto Transit Commission (TTC) has won the American Public Transportation Association's (APTA) Safety Award for safe driving for eighteen out of the last twenty-one years.[354] Its system of rewards for safe driving is likely part of the reason for this remarkable record. (The TTC also uses rewards to help control vandalism. Signs in the trains say: 'Up to $250 reward for information leading to the conviction of anyone removing, defacing or wilfully damaging TTC property or advertising materials.') One obvious reward is winning the APTA award itself. Another is that the division (there are ten in Metro) with the best safety record receives the Silver Shield award. These rewards would probably not be enough to generate the TTC's record of safety. The TTC's safety program would seem to have been successful because of a competition – 'Safety Bingo' – within each division. Each driver has a regular bingo card, and every day a new bingo number is drawn. As in regular bingo, the drivers start filling up their cards. The first driver within the division to get a line completed gets a small token prize, such as a tumbler. The first one to complete two lines gets a somewhat more elaborate prize, such as a flashlight. Completing three lines will win a toaster, and so on. There are also bonus prizes, such as black and white television sets.

Now comes the critical point. One accident by a driver that is that driver's fault, and causes the driver to be off work for more than that day, wipes out not only that person's bingo card but *all* the other bingo cards in the division. Everyone must start the game again with a clean card. So the person with the accident is letting down perhaps 300 other drivers, many of whom might have been close to winning a prize.

The technique, which is used by many companies with various modifications (for example, some use a game called 'steeplechase' and some 'safety poker'),[355] combines a number of features that would seem to help decrease accidents. Perhaps most important, it gives drivers a reason for thinking about safety while they are driving. A recent study by a psychology instructor at the University of Waterloo has shown that even impaired drivers can drive more carefully if given a small incentive to do so. Vogel-Sprott tested the ability of legally impaired young drivers to operate a 'tracometer' (a machine similar to the video games common today) when given twenty-five cents if they performed their task well. Impaired drivers given the monetary incentive performed on a par with a group that had been given a placebo in place of alcohol and no monetary reward.[356]

Peer pressure in the TTC's scheme adds an incentive to be

careful. Some criticize the technique as a management gimmick to reduce compensation claims. (The TTC would have a
particularly strong incentive to reduce claims because it
must fully reimburse the Workers' Compensation scheme
for every claim paid.) Terry Ison, former chair of the British
Columbia Workers' Compensation Board, has written that
such a program is 'a gimmick type of safety program which
creates incentives ... for workers, to reduce recorded claims,
possibly by creating peer group influence not to make a
claim.'[357] No doubt peer pressure operates in this way as
well as in making workers more safety conscious, but overall, as in the case of drunk driving, examined above, peer
pressure, when it can be directed to traffic safety ends, has
an important potential to change behaviour.

The modesty of the actual rewards may in fact enhance
the behavioural effect of the reward program. As psychologist Gerald Wilde, a leading advocate of rewards in driving, has stated:

> The efficacy of relatively small incentives for road safety ...
> may possibly be explained by reference to the theory of
> cognitive dissonance (Festinger 1964). If drivers can be in-
> duced to engage – even temporarily – in new behaviour in
> order to earn an incentive, their attitudes and subsequent
> behaviour will change accordingly. The effects of such tem-
> porary commitments will be larger as the incentive or exter-
> nal justification offered is smaller. When the incentive is
> small, individuals themselves must justify their new behavi-
> our so that it is consistent with the behaviour they are en-
> gaged in.[358]

Psychologist Scott Geller, another leading proponent of
rewards, argues, with reference to B.F. Skinner, that rewards
create a positive attitude in the driver: 'Positive attitudes
associated with a change in behavior maximize the possibility that the desired behavior will become a norm – the so-

cially accepted rule of action. Positive attitudes are apt to follow incentive/reward techniques, since this positive reinforcement approach is generally perceived as "voluntary" and does not elicit perceived threats to individual freedom.'[359]

Geller has done considerable work in connection with the giving of rewards for the use of seat-belts. In various programs he has been able to increase the use of seat-belts through voluntary compliance by means of incentives at locations such as automotive plants, an army ammunition plant, and naval shipyards.[360] An incentive program at the General Motors (GM Technical Center, for example, influenced a 100 per cent increase in safety-belt wearing among 6,000 employees, from a 36 per cent baseline to an average of 70 per cent during the last month of the program, remaining at 60 per cent even before compulsory legislation.[361] A recent article concludes: 'Results across the various corporate-based studies showed that most gains from baseline to intervention periods exceeded 100 per cent, indicating that incentives work remarkably well to motivate safety belt use in industrial settings.'[362]

The GM Technical Laboratories program used a number of interesting techniques to motivate compliance. First, employees signed cards pledging to use seat-belts, a technique employed successfully by groups as diverse as fund-raisers and Alcoholics Anonymous. Second, card signers were eligible for a chance at sweepstake prizes (money and paid vacations). This raises the question whether it is better to get a sure, small prize or a chance at a larger prize. Finally, peer pressure was placed on the potential participants because the sweepstakes would not be held until a designated overall level of seat-belt use was achieved (at first, 60 per cent).[363]

More recent studies by Geller and his associates have, however, raised serious questions about whether incentives are as effective as educational sessions among groups of employees.[364] One study by Geller's group of different programs designed to increase employees' use of safety belts in a large pharmaceutical plant unexpectedly found that incentives and pledges did not increase the use rate of those involved in awareness sessions: 'Groups receiving no incentives and no opportunity to make a safety belt pledge actually showed greater increases in shoulder belt wearing than did their counterparts who received opportunities to win incentive prizes and/or signed commitment pledge cards.'[365] A large-scale study by Geller and others of twenty-eight different programs at nine work settings (including the one at the pharmaceutical plant) came to the same conclusions, which, the authors state, 'were not predicted and are inconsistent with basic reinforcement theory': 'An unexpected and provocative finding of this review, suggesting a critical need for further research, is the greater impact of no-reward strategies from both an immediate and long-term perspective.'[366] 'We currently do not know,' the report states, 'if employees should be offered an extrinsic incentive for making a buckle-up commitment.'[367]

Incentive programs for seat-belt use have also been applied to urban communities. A six-month program in a city of 50,000 in North Carolina in 1983 (before compulsory legislation) using giveaways of small value ($3 to $5) and six monthly draws for a $500 prize, plus a $1,000 grand prize, increased usage from 24 per cent to 41 per cent in the last week of the study. This later dropped to 36 per cent after the program was abandoned.[368]

Some insurance companies have been offering substantial discounts to insureds whose vehicles are equipped with airbags or automatic belts.[369] A US Congressman has proposed the incentive of a tax refund to purchasers of cars with automatic seat-belts.[370]

Gerald Wilde cites,[371] as do others,[372] an experiment in California conducted in the early 1970s involving a free one-year extension of one's driver's licence if there were no accidents or violations. According to Wilde, the results are ambivalent, at best. In one part of the study a group of drivers was promised a one-year free extension if records remained clean during the following year. This group, as it turned out, had 10 per cent more accidents than the control group. In another part of the study a group of persons who had collisions or violations in the previous year were offered a free one-year extension for a clean record in the following year. In this case, the group had 22 per cent fewer accidents than the control group. Both experiments promised a benefit for good driving, and so it is hard to distinguish them. Perhaps the second offered a more substantial benefit, in that it deferred retaking of the written part of the examination for a year, no doubt thought to be a significant benefit for those who had accidents or violations in the previous year.[373] Or perhaps both groups demonstrated regression to the mean.

Wilde also discusses a West German program involving the drivers of the German branch of Kraft Foods Corp. The drivers were told in 1957 that they would receive a bonus of about $150 for every half-year of driving without accidents for which they were at fault. The accident rate dropped dramatically and by 1981 was apparently only 14 per cent of the 1956 rate. The program's results seem impressive, but, as Wilde points out, it contained educational elements in addition to the incentives, and there were no control data from other companies lacking an incentive system.[374]

One area where rewards have been used extensively is in insurance premium reductions for good driving. (Insurance rate changes can also be viewed as penalties.) The subject of insurance was examined more fully above. It is touched on here with specific reference to incentives. Surcharge/discount schemes that have been implemented in Europe and in British Columbia are described by the Slater Task Force on Insurance.[375] British Columbia, for example, adopts a sliding scale for premiums, increasing the rate if there are culpable accidents and decreasing the rate each year if the driver is claim-free.[376] It is, of course, easier to introduce such a scheme with a state-run auto insurance system. Quebec has a state-run, no-fault scheme for personal injuries, paid by a flat levy on drivers, and there is no experience rating.[377] Collision damage to one's own car is handled by private insurance companies, however, and coverage rates for this insurance will vary with accidents and violations.

There is great scope for further exploration of and experimentation with rewards in driving.[378] A government could, for example, introduce a scheme eliminating fees for licence renewals (either for the driver or the vehicle) for accident-free driving. Or, in a government-run insurance scheme, communities could be offered financial incentives if claims against the fund are less than a stated amount. Gerald Wilde suggested such a plan for the province of Saskatchewan (promising payments to young drivers as a group to the extent that they saved the government insurance scheme more than a stated amount), but it was never implemented.[379] It has the advantage of an incentive with a certain degree of peer pressure. Safe driving could be linked with the provincial lottery. A province could, for example, give a violation-free or an accident-free driver one or more provincial lottery tickets every, say, three months. There are a great number of possibilities that could be explored, using licence fees, insurance, lotteries, as well as cash payments, tax deductions or credits, public health-care premium reductions, and so on. What are particularly needed are more controlled experiments in which the efficacy of rewards can be more rigorously tested.[380]

4
Licensing

Licensing is a flexible form of administrative regulation that can be used to impose 'a closer surveillance on conduct'[381] and to demand higher standards of conduct than obtained through the use of criminal or civil sanctions. Licensing techniques can be used in the traffic safety context to control the entry of drivers, to survey and record driving misconduct, and to control and sanction driving activity. Licensing, as a means both to control entry and to enforce exit in response to post-licensing behaviour, is related to the use of education to influence driver behaviour. Education, which will be discussed in the next chapter, can be required as a condition of obtaining a licence and as a post-licensing treatment under the threat of licence suspension.

Licence suspensions remain a frequently used and apparently effective sanction, but the licensing process also provides a means to administer less drastic and more gradual treatments. Such treatments include warning letters, post-licensing driver improvement education, and restrictions on the type of driving undertaken. Licensing will thus clearly play a central role in compliance-based systems of social control.

Targeting High-Risk Subgroups

A common dilemma in devising most traffic safety interventions is that of achieving the optimal balance between interventions that target the entire driving population and those that target drivers who can be identified as subgroups of the driving population who present a high risk of traffic accidents. This dilemma is particularly acute in the use of licensing, education, and exposure-limiting control strategies, because the interventions that seem most feasible and effective, such as licence suspensions for drivers with multiple convictions of driving offences, the raising of minimum driving or drinking ages, and high insurance prices for high-risk drivers, target only a relatively small proportion of the population at risk.

More broadly targeted interventions, such as increasing educative and testing requirements for all to obtain a licence or restricting overall availability of alcohol or fuel, seem either relatively ineffective or else impractical. For example, empirical studies suggest few grounds for believing that the testing of eyesight or other physical characteristics of all drivers can significantly contribute to traffic safety.[382] Likewise, the presence or absence of routine in-person vision and knowledge retesting of drivers for licence renewals seems to have no significant effects on subsequent accident experience.[383] Although evidence suggests that increases in overall economic performance and the pricing of alcohol are significantly correlated with traffic accidents,[384] it is doubtful that society will impose costs such as lower economic performance or large increases in alcohol prices on itself for the sake of traffic safety. Instead those interventions most likely to gain acceptance are those that reduce driving and drinking exposure for small subgroups, such as teenagers or those with poor driving records.

Traffic safety interventions that target high-risk subgroups of the population can influence those drivers who present a high accident risk and can reduce traffic fatalities among the targeted group. Nevertheless, they have limitations as a control of the total traffic safety problem. Traffic offence convictions and demerit points can roughly correlate with future accident experience,[385] but this is complicated because those who drive more have more convictions and accidents.[386] The predictive ability of the correlations is, often, not strong enough to justify drastic interventions, and such interventions can be criticized as an unfair tax on those who drive more. Moreover, it is doubtful that interventions tied to demerit point levels significantly reduce traffic accidents in aggregate terms. Licensing interventions tied to the accumulation of demerit points should be seen as forms of specific deterrence: they target the behaviour of that subgroup already convicted of traffic offences.

Epidemiologists Leon Robertson and Susan Baker studied the prior violations of a sample of drivers fatally injured in automobile accidents and found that more than 50 per cent had no traffic convictions in the three years prior to the fatal crash and that an additional 25 per cent had only one such conviction. Only 5 per cent of those fatally injured had more than three convictions.[387] From these observations, they concluded that even if intensive and successful strategies changed the behaviour of drivers with numerous traffic convictions, only marginal improvements could be achieved in traffic safety.

Other studies have likewise noted the limited effectiveness of even perfectly effective interventions tied to conviction experience. Peck et al. found that even using optimal predictive models, three male drivers with multiple convictions would have to be removed from the road for three years in order to prevent one accident, and 4.4 similar female drivers would have to be removed to prevent one accident over the same period.[388] They dismissed the feasibility of implementing such overinclusive strategies through the state control of licensing and suggested that perhaps insurance companies might make some use of the fairly weak ability of past convictions to predict future accidents. These calculations suggest important limits on the potential effectiveness of interventions that target only an identified high-risk subgroup. Such interventions are dramatically underinclusive of the total driving population at risk while also being significantly overinclusive, in targeting many drivers who despite past convictions and accidents will not have accidents in the future.

Traffic accidents are infrequent probabilistic events not easily predicted on the basis of past behaviour such as con-victions or accidents. Some evidence also suggests that traffic convictions, which are often, as in demerit point systems, used as the predicate for specific deterrence strate-gies, may be given not for the driving behaviour that plays the most important role in accidents but rather for behavi-our that the police can easily apprehend and enforce.[389] The relatively weak ability of past driving behaviour to predict future accidents suggests that traffic accidents should be viewed as not 'a direct behavioural measure but a stochastic consequence of many interactive events' and that 'driving behaviour and accident frequency are not highly corre-lated.'[390]

Such a conclusion should not, of course, be taken as proof that interventions directed toward driving behaviour cannot have traffic safety benefits. Interventions directed toward high-risk drivers can indeed increase traffic safety at the margins. At the same time, however, we have found that the limitations of many interventions targeting high-risk drivers have often not been adequately recognized in the research and policy literature.

Targeting Teenagers

Young drivers, since they are disproportionately involved in accidents, are the frequent focus for special control strategies. It is not clear whether their over-representation in accidents can be explained primarily through their inexperience with driving or through behavioural and environmental factors such as aggression, immaturity, and peer pressure specific to young people.

To the extent that driving inexperience contributes to young drivers' accidents, interventions that reduce teenage driving exposure will have substantial offsetting effects through postponement of driving experience. To the extent that immaturity and related factors such as desire for and perceptions of risks[391] contribute to young drivers' accidents, interventions that limit teenagers' exposure will be more effective in reducing traffic accidents by preventing or reducing the driving of some of our most dangerous drivers. Most likely both the inexperience and immaturity hypotheses have some explanatory value. Interventions that target young drivers can prevent accidents, but there may be offsetting effects when teenagers begin to drive at an older age.

Recent changes in the minimum legal drinking age in most North American jurisdictions have facilitated the accumulation of knowledge concerning the effects that raising and lowering the drinking age can have on traffic accidents. Other licensing techniques directed at teenagers include changing the minimum legal age for obtaining a driver's licence, probationary or graduated licences, night-time curfews, and other restrictions on newly licensed drivers.

The consensus of studies has been that the reductions made in the legal minimum drinking age in the 1970s were associated with increases in youthful traffic fatalities. Cook and Tauchen concluded from a study of twenty instances in which the drinking age was lowered from twenty-one to eighteen that traffic fatalities among that age group rose, on average, by 7 per cent. Traffic fatalities also increased among sixteen-to-seventeen-year-olds, but to a lesser extent.[392]

Conversely, research suggests that increasing the minimum legal drinking age will reduce automobile accidents among affected age groups. On the basis of these findings, US federal highway funds are withheld from any state that does not adopt a twenty-one-year-old minimum legal drinking age. Williams et al. conclude from data on nine states in which the drinking age was raised from eighteen to twenty-one that a 41 per cent reduction in night-time, single-vehicle fatal crashes among the affected population occurred.[393] Subsequent studies are somewhat less optimistic, one predicting between 8 and 18 per cent fewer fatal crash involvements for night-time drivers from raising the minimum drinking age.[394] Saffer and Grossman have predicted that a uniform twenty-one-year legal minimum drinking age could have produced an 8 per cent reduction in eighteen- to twenty-one-year-old traffic fatalities between 1975 and 1981.[395] When the legal drinking age was raised from eighteen to nineteen in Ontario, however, no significant reductions in total traffic fatalities or drunk driving convictions were observed in the following year,[396] but these anomalous findings seem to be related to the minimal one-year change and gradual phasing in of the new higher minimum drinking age.[397]

A hypothesis has been presented that a higher drinking age merely postpones the dangerous period in which inexperienced drinkers drive,[398] but this hypothesis is challenged by evidence that many 'underage' adolescents gain experience with both drinking and driving[399] and by rival interpretations of the base data.[400] The traffic safety effectiveness of a higher minimum legal drinking age is achieved not by directly targeting behaviour that combines drinking and driving or even by preventing underage teenagers from drinking, but probably by limiting the frequency and influencing the location of alcohol consumption.[401] Hence the higher age seems to operate as a non-punitive compliance technique, as opposed to a prosecution-based sanction.

The impact of the minimum legal drinking age is

mediated through the desire and ability of licensed servers and vendors of alcohol to enforce the minimum drinking age, although the simple existence of a higher minimum drinking age may also have an effect. Servers and vendors of alcohol are also in a position to regulate the drinking of all potential drivers, but it is not known how effective such regulation is or could be in preventing drinking and driving. In a pattern that appears throughout the licensing field, more support is available for interventions that target high-risk subgroups than those directed at the entire population at risk. There is a willingness to restrict availability to alcohol for teenagers, but any broader application of this technique is often criticized as an unacceptable form of neo-prohibition.[402]

Not surprisingly, raising the minimum age for obtaining a driver's licence can significantly reduce traffic accidents in the age group that cannot obtain a licence. For example, one study has determined that in New Jersey, where the minimum age for obtaining a licence is seventeen years of age, the fatality rate of sixteen-year-old drivers is 4 per 100,000 population, whereas in Connecticut with a sixteen-year-old minimum, the rate is 26 fatalities per 100,000 population of sixteen-year-olds. At the same time, however, the slightly higher fatality rates of seventeen-year-olds in New Jersey suggest that the benefits of the higher New Jersey age may be partially offset, probably because sixteen-year-olds in that state cannot as easily gain driving experience.[403] In general, traffic safety measures designed to reduce exposure to driving or drinking seem to reduce accidents, although sacrifice of experience may cause some offsetting effects.

Most jurisdictions require those learning to drive to obtain a learner's permit which is often accompanied by restrictions, such as requiring the presence of an adult licensed driver and prohibiting night-time driving. After a licence is obtained, young drivers are typically placed in probationary programs through which interventions such as warning letters, driver improvement education, and licence suspensions are triggered by the recording of convictions or accidents. Evaluations of such programs suggest that they may reduce both convictions and accidents, probably by encouraging some unknown combination of increased care and reduced driving activity.[404]

Some researchers believe that greater potential exists for graduated licensing programs that impose strategic restrictions on the driving of *all* new drivers and that do not focus only on those who are recorded by the police as involved in convictions or accidents.[405] Driving restrictions under such graduated licensing programs could include night-time and/or weekend curfews, requirements that adults accompany young drivers, prohibitions on young drivers transporting other teenagers, and lower levels of prohibited blood alcohol concentrations for young drivers. Despite the potential of graduated licences to help all young drivers gain experience in a manner that restricts risk, most licensing interventions directed at young drivers target only those with accidents or record convictions. Once again, more support is available for interventions that target high-risk subgroups identified through the criminal justice system than those that target more broadly defined populations.

The licensing process can be used to impose restrictions on the type of driving. Night-time curfews on young drivers may reduce traffic fatalities among the affected population. One study has concluded after comparing accident rates in states in which night-time driving curfews were and were not imposed, that curfews on sixteen-year-olds reduced their crash involvement by as much as 69 per cent in Pennsylvania, 62 per cent in New York, 40 per cent in Maryland, and 25 per cent in Louisiana.[406] Some of these results have, however, been challenged, and another researcher has suggested that the reduction in Maryland fatalities is the product of long-term trends, independent of the 1 a.m. to 6 a.m. curfew imposed on probationary drivers in that state.[407]

Despite these reservations, the night-time curfew may reduce exposure of young drivers in high-risk periods, but further experiments with implementation and evaluation are needed.

Other possible restrictions on young drivers are to require that they drive with another adult licensed driver, parent or guardian, and to prohibit them from transporting other teenagers. An American study suggests that over 90 per cent of vehicles in fatal crashes driven by male drivers and over 75 per cent driven by female drivers under eighteen had no adult passengers and that teenagers, especially women, are disproportionately present as passengers injured or killed in automobile crashes involving teenage drivers.[408] Restrictions requiring adults and prohibiting teenagers in cars driven by teenagers may reduce traffic accidents, either by decreased exposure or through the ability of the adult to regulate or influence driving practices. As in most traffic safety interventions, there may be harmful and offsetting substitution effects: more adults could be involved in accidents as passengers, and more teenagers could be killed or injured driving their own cars or as pedestrians.

Higher minimum driving or drinking ages and night-time curfews seem to reduce traffic accidents. They operate primarily by reducing the driving activity of the affected population and its exposure to alcohol, but teenagers may exercise greater care when avoiding these prohibitions and such care may prevent some accidents. All these interventions may induce some offsetting effects, but it is doubtful that the harmful effects of inexperience at older ages will cancel out the advantages of reduced exposure at younger ages.

Post-Licensing Control

In almost all jurisdictions, licence suspensions are used as a sanction of last resort. Typically, drivers with poor records of traffic violations receive warning letter(s) and/or driver improvement courses before their licences are suspended. The gradual nature of the sanctioning process attached to licensing is intuitively appealing, as it creates the potential for early preventive interventions as a driver begins to accumulate demerit points. The effectiveness of the various licensing interventions has not been sufficiently evaluated, but the results of existing research suggest that the most effective intervention is the rather drastic sanction of licence suspension. Licence suspension can be made less severe by use of shorter or intermittent terms and by special allowance for occupational requirements. Licence suspension prevents accidents, even though many suspended drivers continue to drive. Licence suspension acts as an effective traffic safety measure through the threat of its imposition, by reducing driving activity and perhaps even by increasing the care a suspended driver takes when driving illegally.[409]

Few positive traffic safety results, in the form of significant reductions in subsequent accidents, have been observed from the use of warning letters, but they are generally seen to be a cost-effective intervention.[410] Mixed results have been achieved from individual or group driver improvement interventions, with some being shown to change knowledge and attitudes and reduce traffic convictions, but less frequently to reduce accidents.[411] Licence suspensions have generally proved effective in reducing convictions or accidents during their imposition, although significant numbers of drivers subject to this sanction often continue to drive, record convictions, and be involved in crashes. One recent survey of three evaluation studies has concluded from California data that multiple drunk-driving offenders receiving long-term suspensions in addition to fines and/or sentences had 'at least 30% fewer accidents and convictions than similar drivers receiving only fines and/or jail sentences.'[412] It is not known what combination of reduced driving activity or increased levels of care[413] account for the improvement. The effectiveness of licence suspensions for multiple traffic

offenders as opposed to convicted drunk drivers has, however, been more ambiguous.[414]

Greater attention should be paid to the use of short-term
licence suspensions. By reducing the severity of licence
suspensions, this intervention can be imposed more frequently and on a wider range of drivers. A recent study,
using the Michigan probationary licence program, compared the effects of both the threat and the imposition of a
short, fourteen-day licence suspension with the threat and
imposition of an individual interview designed to diagnose
and change safety errors made by a particular driver. The
threat of the short suspension seemed significantly to reduce
both subsequent traffic violations and accidents for women
over a two-year period, with only the actual imposition of
the suspension producing reductions in traffic violations
and accidents for men and at a less significant rate than for
women. Moreover, a short licence suspension, estimated to
cost $3 per imposition, was significantly more cost-effective
than a diagnostic interview costing $70 per imposition.[415]
Likewise, in most evaluated studies, licence suspensions
have proved more effective in reducing accidents than more
costly educational programs.[416]

In general, the most effective licensing control strategies
are those, such as higher minimum driving and drinking
ages, night-time curfews, and licence suspensions, that
operate primarily by reducing exposure. Although these
interventions probably operate primarily by reducing driving activity as opposed to increasing care levels, their ability
to increase care levels through the desire of drivers to avoid
apprehension while driving or drinking illegally should be
carefully examined. Targeting teenagers by increasing the
minimum legal ages of driving or drinking seems to reduce
traffic fatalities among the affected population, but less
drastic interventions, such as use of restricted licences,
night-time curfews, and the imposition of liability on those
who serve teenagers alcohol, may also reduce traffic acci-

dents. Licensing demerit point systems can identify drivers who present an above-average accident risk, but, within the group identified, it appears that only a minority of drivers will actually have accidents in the future and that that sub-group will constitute a minority of the overall population of drivers who will have accidents. These observations place important limits on the impact of specific deterrence interventions triggered by accumulation of demerit points.

should, at best, supplement licence suspensions. Given this, it is especially important to subject educative interventions to cost-effectiveness scrutiny.

Employer-Implemented Educational Programs

Employers may be in an excellent position to provide incentives to influence their employees' behaviour. As noted earlier, employers have been able to induce the wearing of seat-belts through use of reward strategies. Employer-implemented educational programs directed at employees have also resulted in impressive increases (152–285 per cent) in seat-belt usage which seem to persist longer than those gained from the use of reward strategies.[431] This suggests that educative strategies may even be better at inducing long-term behavioural change than the short-term effects of offering rewards.

Alcoholism treatment in response to poor job performance also has potential to reduce drunk and reckless driving convictions and total collisions.[432] As with employers, high schools may be in an advantageous position to control the behaviour of their students, but, as of yet, evaluations of school-based programs for prevention of drinking and driving have suggested that such interventions can increase knowledge and change attitudes only over the short term.[433] More attention needs to be paid to the effectiveness of education in changing driving behaviour and the subsequent effectiveness of any changes in driving behaviour in reducing traffic accidents. Use of employers to implement non-punitive compliance strategies such as rewards and education, however, is a method of social control with significant potential.

Mass Media

Most researchers have concluded that mass media campaigns rarely influence behaviour, although they may convey information and even change attitudes. Extensive use of television commercials has not been shown in controlled experiments to change behaviour such as seat-belt use.[434] Studies also suggest that advertising of alcohol does not have significant effects on aggregate or individual levels of consumption[435] and suggest that prohibitions on alcohol advertising are not likely to reduce drunk driving by decreasing alcohol consumption. Such prohibitions may, however, have a symbolic value that can complement socio-cultural forms of social control.

Mass media campaigns are often used to publicize new laws and enforcement campaigns. Although mere passage and publicity of laws requiring seat-belt use seem to affect usage, most experience suggests that publicity concerning laws or enforcement campaigns alone will not change drunk driving or reduce alcohol-related accidents.[436] A publicity campaign in Edmonton, Alberta, was, however, apparently successful: it was associated with reduced drunk driving as measured by roadside surveys compared to the control city of Calgary. The Edmonton campaign did not try directly to change attitudes or behaviour; it concentrated on supplying information that would be useful to drivers, such as the number of drinks required to reach illegal blood alcohol concentrations.[437] Some pressure groups, however, object to information campaigns that convey information on a 'safe' amount of alcohol that can be consumed before driving[438] because they believe it undermines the stigmatization of drinking and driving. Yet given the widespread occurrence of behaviour that combines drinking and driving,[439] it may be better to provide potential drunk drivers with useful information rather than to rely on either exaggerated fears of apprehension or the simplistic moral edict – if you drink, don't drive.

Although publicity alone seems unlikely to change behaviour in ways that will affect traffic accidents, use of mass media seems to play a crucial role, as a necessary but not sufficient condition, in the short-term success of general deterrence campaigns against drunk driving. Official publicity disseminated as part of an enforcement campaign or obtained unofficially through newspaper reports or through the objections of civil libertarians operates by communicating an increased likelihood of punishment.[440] Publicity can help produce exaggerated perceptions of the likelihood of apprehension and punishment, but the effects of these perceptions on behaviour are likely to erode as drivers learn, through experience, that the likelihood of apprehension remains low.

This review of the findings of the effectiveness of various educational strategies is consistent with the US National Research Council's conclusion that, on the basis of current evidence, educational strategies are less effective than either use of sanctions or regulation of environmental design: 'The tendency to attribute injuries to "human error" has nourished the hope that they can best be prevented through voluntary behaviour change. Yet neither safety-education campaigns nor driver-education programs have been shown by scientific evaluation to justify the faith and large budgets accorded them. Educational and informational programs should be held to the same standards of efficacy as other prophylactic interventions; furthermore, it should not be assumed that such programs cannot do harm.'[441]

This last observation should not be ignored, as the findings reviewed indicate that high school driving education may make those individuals who take it marginally safer drivers, but that its widespread availability will increase automobile accidents by facilitating early licensing and increased exposure among more teenagers. Furthermore, rehabilitative programs may have negative traffic safety implications if they are used to replace, rather than supplement, more effective interventions, such as licence suspensions. In general, exposure-limiting devices seem to yield better traffic safety results, by reducing activity levels, than educative interventions designed to persuade drivers to take more care when driving.

PART TWO

Environment-Centred
Counter-measures

6

Economic Variables

A New Theory

Recent research has raised the controversial possibility that a significant percentage, indeed perhaps the overwhelming majority, of traffic accidents can be explained by factors outside the conventional causal matrix of driver error and motor vehicle, highway, and environmental design in the Haddon framework.

General economic trends, operating through such variables as gas prices, unemployment, reduced rates of increase in real incomes, and perhaps the fleet mix, are argued to have a major effect on traffic accident figures. The worldwide oil crisis in 1973, the recession that followed, the recession of the late 1970s and early 1980s, and the dramatic reductions in traffic fatality figures that accompanied them underlined how sensitive these figures are to economic influences. This suggests the effect of activity levels and their economic determinants, as well as of driver error and failure in the design of vehicles and highways, on accident levels. The role of activity levels was intuitively obvious from the turn of the century: as the automobile became popularized, accidents increased dramatically, but their importance was often obscured by attention to the conventional causal matrix. Even the much less conventional and expansive Haddon matrix does not take account of activity levels. It is principally the recent work of economists that has focused attention on the importance of activity levels for traffic safety.

Activity (how much driving is engaged in) will be determined by economic factors that influence the demand for driving. As for any other normal economic good, demand will be a function of the price of the activity (the price elasticity of demand) and the income of demanders (the income elasticity of demand). If the price of driving significantly increases, as it did with gas price increases following the OPEC oil price shocks in 1973 and 1979, demand will fall, with the decrease being most pronounced among the most price elastic (sensitive) demanders. If real incomes fall, through increases in unemployment and decreases in productivity, as they did for many individuals in the recession following the oil crisis of 1973 and again in the much more severe recession of the late 1970s and early 1980s, demands for driving will decrease, especially among the most income elastic (sensitive) demanders. A countervailing safety effect is a likely increase in the demand for smaller, more fuel-efficient cars, which are significantly more hazardous to occupants in the event of collisions than larger cars.[442]

This economic model of determinants of levels of driving activity could not be more rudimentary. What remains to be seen is how well it predicts or explains changes not only in driving activity but also in accident rates. At one level the implications of the model are uncontroversial. Obviously, accidents are correlated to a large extent with miles driven. The total number of traffic accidents or fatalities annually in the United States, one might conjecture, would be roughly about ten times the total number of accidents or fatalities in Canada, reflecting the difference in population sizes of, and volume of driving in, the two countries. This conjecture is borne out by the evidence. Risk exposure would similarly explain why the total number of accidents would fall in an economic environment of rapid price increases, especially for gasoline, and rising unemployment.

However, it would not, without more, explain why accident (or fatality) rates (per distance) would also fall. Here, the activity level hypothesis of the determinants of accident frequency moves to a somewhat more subtle level. It hypothesizes not only a reduction in the total quantity of driving but qualitative shifts in the nature of driving in response to price increases and income reduction. In particular, it conjectures that 'discretionary' driving and related activities will be reduced more sharply than 'non-discretionary' driving and that 'discretionary' driving entails driving with higher levels of risk exposure, such as certain forms of vacation driving or driving to and from dinners or parties often entailing alcohol consumption, and that economically more marginal categories or drivers who are likely to be most sensitive to gas price increases and most affected by increases in unemployment will reduce their driving most. To the extent that high-risk groups of drivers (e.g. young men) are over-represented in these economically more marginal categories, reductions in their level of driving activity may reduce accident (or fatality) rates.

Empirical Evidence

Most of the empirical research is very recent, is in some respects still quite tentative, and is widely viewed as raising difficult and controversial problems of interpretation.

The most widely cited study is that undertaken by Partyka.[443] She employs a simple employment model in which fatalities are the dependent variable and the independent variables are unemployed workers, employed workers, and those not a part of the labour force (together the three groups account for the entire adult population). The model is fitted to yearly US traffic fatality data from 1960 to 1982.

This model explains 89 per cent of the variability in fatalities during this period.

The model began to 'stray' from the data in 1974, when the oil embargo caused shortages and price increases. At the same time, the US government introduced the national 55-mph speed limit on all highways. Partyka modified her model to take account of these two factors. The amended model explains 98 per cent of the variability in fatalities since 1960. The oil embargo was found to have decreased fatalities by 3,995 in 1974, and the speed limit decreased fatalities by 4,824 per year. Other year-to-year variations in fatality levels are apparently explained by income effects.

Hedlund et al,[444] in a more detailed version of Partyka's model, used a number of possible alternatives to employment statistics, regressing monthly US fatality data from 1975–82 on vehicle miles of travel (VMT), the Federal Reserve Board's production index, personal income, and retail sales, and found that all work equally well as explanators of variations in fatalities. Hedlund concludes that the four variables measure roughly the same thing – VMT (exposure or activity levels) – and the latter three variables serve as proxies for this. These models predict about two-thirds of the 1980–2 fatality decrease. Economic activity variables explain youth fatalities better than non-youth fatalities for this period, suggesting that youth are more affected than others by economic change.

While these economic or activity level models explained or predicted fatality levels with impressive accuracy from 1960 to 1982, the economic recovery that began in early 1983 would have suggested an increase in fatalities as the recovery gathered strength and risk exposure and driving activity levels increased. However, total fatalities continued to drop sharply (from 51,091 in 1980 to 42,000 in 1983 – a 17 per cent decrease – and continue to fall). Thus, the model substantially overpredicts fatality levels in the last several years. Hedlund[445] attributes a small portion of recent de-

creases to a marginal increase in seat-belt use and a larger
portion to less alcohol involvement in fatal accidents, presumably as a result of drunk driving crackdowns or changing attitudes to drinking and driving. However, a significant
residual remains unexplained.

Hedlund concludes that the 1980–3 fatality drop can be
attributed primarily to behavioural factors, not changes in
vehicles, roads, or other influences. In fact, overall travel
rose 8 per cent over this period: 'Economic conditions
appear to have influenced the behavioral factors, though it is
still unclear just how this influence took place ... Hard data
to analyze and disaggregate the behavioral changes are
scant. In particular, travel miles by driver age, time of day,
or trip purpose would be most useful but are unavail-
able.'[446]

Adams is prepared to offer a conjecture as to how the
state of the economy may influence behaviour:

> It is possible that not only exposure to risk, but also attitudes
> toward risk might vary with the state of the economy. It has
> been noted (e.g. Toffler, *The Third Wave*, 1980) that a great
> many things – from fashions in dress to sexual mores – vary
> with ups and downs of the economy. One might speculate,
> with the help of the Risk Homeostasis Theory, that in times of
> economic prosperity life in general seems more secure, and
> people spend a greater proportion of their risk budgets on
> voluntarily selected risks, while in bad times, when people
> feel more at risk economically, they attempt to maintain their
> target levels of risk by cutting down on risk of a more volun-
> tary nature.[447]

This explanation, apart from being wholly conjectural,
also is not able to explain the continuing drop in fatality
rates since the beginning of US economic recovery in early
1983. Moreover, Adams's reliance on the risk reduction
explanation of accident trends creates some tension with his

explanation of the secular decline in fatality rates in many industrialized economies (referred to as 'Smeed's Law'), which Adams attributes to a learning-curve effect induced by greater exposure. It is difficult to espouse simultaneously risk reduction and learning-curve explanations for accident trends.

Hedlund's explanation of the secular decline in fatality rates is not much more convincing. He casually ascribes it to 'roads, vehicles, emergency care, number of teenage drivers, and other components of the traffic system (that) are changing gradually and share the credit for the long-term fatality rate decline.'[448]

Policy Implications

The direct policy implications for traffic safety of the Partyka line of analysis are not obvious: inducing economic recessions to reduce traffic accidents is not a helpful prescription. However, the indirect policy implications of an emphasis on activity levels and exposure variables are of considerable importance.[449] As we have already seen in licensing, the terms on which licences are granted or withdrawn can affect accident rates; similarly in the case of availability of alcohol.

Beyond these direct attempts to regulate exposure, the evidence reviewed here suggests the importance of harnessing pricing mechanisms to reduce activity levels and hence exposure.[450] As we saw in the impact of tort-insurance regimes on accident rates, pricing high-risk drivers off the highways through differentiated insurance premiums may well significantly affect accident rates. Saffer and Grossman[451] also estimate that a policy that fixed the US federal beer tax in real terms since 1951 and that taxed the alcohol in beer at the same rates as the alcohol in liquor would have reduced fatalities among eighteen-to-twenty-year-olds by 54 per cent between 1975 and 1981. Raising gasoline taxes to reflect otherwise non-internalized accident costs (e.g. costs to the health care system) may further reduce activity levels.[452] And, finally, adjusting relative prices of private motoring and public transit so as to reflect externalities associated with the former may again influence activity levels in appropriate ways. However effective this class of policies may be in promoting traffic safety, in some cases there will be strong political resistance from the groups targeted for special constraints or costs and ethical objections that group definitions will be overinclusive and will penalize low-risk individuals within these groups for ascriptive characteristics over which they have no control.

7

Motor Vehicle Safety Design

Evolution

While safety concerns over particular features of motor vehicle design go back to the early decades of this century,[453] detailed regulation of vehicle safety design is a relatively recent public counter-measure. Some observers date the public policy focus on vehicle design to the publication in 1965 of Ralph Nader's book, *Unsafe at Any Speed*,[454] which purported to expose major safety hazards in the Chevrolet Corvair, and to the public outrage provoked by revelations that General Motors had retained private investigators to tail Nader and delve into his professional and personal life, which produced the needed political climate for regulating the powerful automotive industry.

However, as we saw above, more fundamental intellectual influences pushing in this policy direction reflected epidemiologically oriented theories of injuries, which had become increasingly prominent in the 1950s and 1960s under the stimulus of research and writing by American scholars such as Hugh DeHaven and William Haddon jr, who emphasized the causes of injuries, rather than of accidents.[455] This epidemiological perspective reflected a belief that science and law together could fashion solutions to safety problems that would transcend human failure.[456] Congress enacted the National Traffic and Motor Vehicle Safety Act[457] in 1966, which set up what has become the National Highway and Traffic Safety Administration (NHTSA), whose first administrator was William Haddon. In Canada, the federal Motor Vehicle Safety Act[458] was enacted in 1971 and is administered by Transport Canada (a department of government). Under both US and Canadian statutes, regulations may specify required safety features in new motor vehicles. Because of the integrated nature of the North American automobile industry, safety design regulations under the two statutes are nearly identical.

Some of the safety standards that have been promulgated are directed to reducing the frequency of accidents, while others are directed to reducing their severity. Six major occupant protection categories account for roughly two-thirds of the costs of safety regulation (excluding the bumper standard, which is mostly intended to reduce motor-vehicle body damage): interior protection (e.g. padded dashes), head restraints, energy-absorbing steering systems, penetration-resistant windscreen glass, seat-belt installations, and side-door beams. Dual braking systems account for most of the costs of the accident prevention standards. These seven categories of standards cover more than three-quarters of the entire cost of safety regulations imposed by NHTSA (excluding bumper standards).[459]

A number of NHTSA assessments[460] and external studies,[461] typically undertaken by engineers, have attempted to estimate the savings in fatalities and bodily injuries from these standards. Substantial savings have generally been reported and have been relied on as vindicating the effectiveness of this class of safety counter-measure.

Joan Claybrook, administrator of NHTSA in the Carter administration, and David Bollier assert that an estimated 10,000 US motorists' lives are saved and tens of thousands of individuals spared injury each year as a result of auto safety regulation.[462] They also argue that prior to regulation the US auto industry invested trivial sums on research and development on safety improvements and was able to exploit the substantial symmetries in information between manufacturers and consumers as to safety hazards posed by design features of automobiles and as to the costs and benefits of alternative designs, to minimize investments in vehicle safety. The industry's public posture was alleged historically to have been that fatalities and injuries sustained in automobile accidents were almost always attributable to 'human factors' – the 'nut behind the wheel' – and promoted a focus on driver education and traffic law enforcement, not safer car design. The authors claim that distinguishing between first and second collisions – largely attributed initially to Haddon – was 'a major analytic breakthrough in the history of automobile safety'[463] and led to more subtle appreciation of the need for different counter-measures for the pre-crash, crash, and post-crash phases of auto accidents.

The recent history of motor vehicle safety regulation in the United States (and derivatively in Canada) has seen a marked shift away from promulgating new safety standards to issuing mandatory recall orders for vehicles suspected of possessing unsafe design features. Almost all major US safety standards were promulgated prior to 1974, whereas motor vehicle recalls have increased from about 15 million vehicles between 1966 and 1970, to about 30 million vehicles from 1971 to 1975, to over 39 million vehicles between 1976 and 1980. Mashaw and Harfst[464] attribute this shift to difficulties that NHTSA has encountered in providing a justificatory record for technology-forcing changes that can withstand judicial review, compared to the relatively relaxed judicial standards that recall orders have been required to meet. This switch in focus from rule making to regulation by recall has occurred despite evidence that vehicle failures account for only a very small percentage of accidents and that most of these are attributable to poor owner maintenance.[465] They argue that significant barriers exist to public regulation of auto design through rule making, despite the apparent superiority of such regulation to recalls in terms of a safety pay-off. We will now focus on the effectiveness of motor vehicle safety standards.

Reaction

A major challenge to the conceptual or causal discreteness of the categories of first and second collisions, or pre-crash, crash, and post-crash phases of accidents, which under-pinned NHTSA's standard-setting mandate was posed by a highly controversial article by Sam Peltzman, a University of Chicago economist, published in 1975.[466] He postulated that by reducing the consequences of the second collision (i.e. the severity of an accident) through safety regulations, 'driving intensity' would be increased as drivers took more risks in order to achieve the same trade-off that they had demanded prior to regulation between expected accident costs and benefits from conserving time on the road. While 'increased private demand for safety and safety regulation will both produce lower costs per accident ... regulation, to the extent that it is independent of the private demand for safety, will produce a higher equilibrium driving intensity for the same reduction in cost per accident.'[467] This hypothesis reflects theories of risk compensation or risk homeostasis that con-tinue to agitate traffic safety researchers over a broad range of issues.

Peltzman set out to test his hypothesis empirically in two ways. First, a time-series analysis was undertaken whereby an equation was fitted to data from 1944 to 1964 (during which period, except in the last several years, there had been a steady secular decline in the fatality rate per vehicle mile). Increases in permanent income (decreasing the fatality rate) and the proportion of young drivers on the road, short-term

increases in real income, vehicle speeds, and alcohol consumption (all increasing the fatality rate), were, in this order,
found to be the most significant variables.

Extrapolating from these variables to predict future fatality rates absent motor vehicle safety regulation, Peltzman
found that predicted fatality rates almost exactly tracked
actual fatality rules with vehicle safety regulation. In short,
regulation had no impact on overall fatality rates. While
occupant fatality rates fell somewhat, fatality rates for
pedestrians, motorcyclists, and cyclists rose by an equivalent
amount. Increased driving by young drivers and an increased incidence of drunk driving offences are identified by
Peltzman as evidence of increased risk-taking offsetting
reduced costs of accidents.

Cross-sectional analysis was also undertaken by Peltzman
to test whether states with a higher proportion of newer cars
with mandated safety features reported lower fatality rates
than states with a higher proportion of pre-regulation vehicles. No such effect was found. In addition, in North Carolina, between 1966 and 1968, the probability of an accident
involving cars with mandated safety devices was 40 per cent
greater than for cars not so equipped.

Peltzman's findings have been strongly contested by other
researchers. Various methodological features of his empirical estimations have been challenged. In particular, Robertson[468] claimed to find that fatality rates per vehicle mile for
vehicles subject to safety regulation for the period 1975–8
were about half those for unregulated vehicles, entailing an
estimated saving of 37,000 lives over the four-year period.

The methodology of Robertson's study in turn has been
severely criticized by Orr,[469] who found that at best one-
fourth of the life-saving effect claimed by Robertson could
be attributed to safety regulation. Most of the effects claimed
by Robertson were attributed by Orr to motor vehicle age (a
vintage effect), with age of vehicles involved in fatal accidents being a dominant explanatory variable both before

and after promulgation of safety regulations and exhibiting no significant variance when or after the regulations came into force. Age of car is hypothesized to be highly and inversely correlated with age of driver (and might be largely a proxy for the latter, that is, on average, the older the car, the younger the driver).

Vindication?

However, the latest study of the impact of motor vehicle safety regulation on fatality and injury rates, recently published by the Brookings Institution and undertaken by Crandall, Gruenspecht, Keeler, and Lave,[470] raises serious doubts about Peltzman's hypothesis, at least in its limiting form, while acknowledging more modest risk compensation effects. While the study reaches harsh judgments on the net economic effects of fuel efficiency and emission regulations, it reaches a highly favourable conclusion on the effects of safety regulation, finding that regulation may have reduced fatalities by as much as 40 per cent since the inception of the program and may entail an annual reduction in fatalities of as many as 23,000 – substantially higher than most previous engineering studies would have implied, and much more than even enthusiastic advocates of safety regulation, such as Claybrook, have been prepared to claim.

The Brookings study, like Peltzman's, contains both time-series and cross-sectional analysis of the determinants of highway fatalities but covers the period 1947–81, which provides nine more years of data on the effect of safety regulations.

Safety improvements in vehicles, effect of truck miles on other highway users, and higher incomes, which increase the value of time and may induce more risk taking, were found to be highly significant variables. Youth, alcohol, and speed were of relatively little significance, while share of miles driven on limited-access highways proved significant

when insignificant regression variables were dropped from
the equation. Vintage effects, independent of other variables,
were found to be negligible. The number of deaths in the
non-occupant and pedestrian cyclist categories was found to
be inversely related to the safety index, but the magnitude of
the coefficients was considerably smaller than the positive
coefficients in the occupants' equation. The effects of youth
and alcohol are more pronounced in the non-occupant, pedestrian, and cyclist categories.

These data provide support for the risk compensation
hypothesis, but not the more extreme risk homeostasis hypothesis. For example, the authors suggest that one could
conclude that actual highway deaths were as many as 10,000
fewer per year by the mid-1970s than might have been expected from a single extrapolation of the 1947–65 experience,
but that non-occupant deaths were as many as 4,000 higher.
Cross-sectional analysis of fatality rates, regressed on safety-
weighted vintage automobile stock indexes for fifty states,
confirmed the significance of safety regulation as a determinant of fatality rates, although offsetting effects on non-
occupants were less consistently discernible.

Having discovered positive (and substantial) benefits
from safety regulation, the Brookings researchers then in-
vestigated whether benefits exceeded costs – irrelevant in
Peltzman's analysis, giving a finding of zero benefits. They
found that benefits substantially exceeded costs, except on
the most pessimistic estimates of benefits and costs. They
acknowledge that their data suggest only that total benefits
appear to be greater than the total costs of safety improvements in cars, not that the marginal benefits of every safety
regulation exceed its marginal costs.

Crandall et al. also evaluate the costs and benefits of long-
standing and controversial proposals to mandate installation
of passive restraint systems (airbags or automatic belts) in
automobiles.[471] With respect to airbags, they estimate annual
cost to be between $2.1 billion and $4.2 billion and benefits

to occupants between $3.3 billion and $16.2 billion. Any value assigned to life in excess of $500,000 would generate net benefits, ignoring feedback effects on new car demand (and hence increased retention of older, unmodified cars) and offsetting driving behaviour. Automatic belts would entail annual costs of $525 million to $1.6 billion dollars and benefits of between $0.7 billion to $11.1 billion – the wide range of benefits reflecting uncertainty over usage rates and detachability.

Blomquist criticizes these and similar estimates for failing to take account of risk compensation and to place a cost on time, inconvenience, and disutility associated with use of the system and thus concludes that estimates of net social benefits are substantially overstated.[472] After protracted public debates, all new automobiles from 1990 on will be required to be fitted with some form of passive restraint system for the driver and by 1993 for all front-seat occupants[473] – unless, of course, there are further delays.

Reservations

First, while the Brookings study seems the most careful and detailed analysis of motor vehicle safety regulation yet undertaken, the authors acknowledge that 'why the estimate [of fatality reductions] is so high frankly remains somewhat of a puzzle.'[474] It is clearly an outlier in relation to all previous studies.

Second, it is not clear that we are any closer to full understanding of risk compensatory adaptive behaviour on the part of vehicle drivers.[475] The Brookings findings strongly rule out completely offsetting adaptive responses to improvements in motor vehicle safety where drivers seek to reinstate predetermined target levels of risk. Moreover, the data seem consistent with the premises of safety regulation – that many design hazards are imperfectly perceived by drivers and occupants and correspondingly that the impact of design regulations on these hazards is also probably imperfectly perceived, so that it seems implausible that drivers are likely to react to imperfectly appreciated reductions in imperfectly appreciated prior risks by acting on their original private demand for particular safety-performance trade-offs. In short, the risk homeostasis hypothesis seems to assume a full information world.

As Lund and O'Neill argue,[476] improved handling characteristics (e.g. better braking capacity, studded tires) of vehicles are likely to generate immediate feedback to drivers and may induce behavioural responses, but design changes that increase occupant protection (e.g. stronger side-door beams) usually provide no direct and immediate feedback and should have little or no effect on driving behaviour. The risk compensation hypothesis in some contexts thus seems much more plausible than a generalized risk homeostasis hypothesis but is also much more untidy: it yields little in the way of a clear theory as to when drivers will engage in adaptive behaviour and to what extent.

Third, even if vehicle safety design regulations do reduce injuries on net, widespread public hostility to the seat-belt ignition interlock requirements promulgated by NHTSA in 1974 and subsequently rescinded, and ongoing protracted debates about the wisdom of alternative passive restraint requirements, raise more general political and ideological questions about the imposition of self-protective requirements, obviously exemplified most prominently by requirements devoted to protection of occupants from the consequences of the 'second collision.' Leading proponents of such requirements, such as DeHaven and Haddon, viewed them as holding out greater safety potential than many alternative safety counter-measures. But in liberal individualistic societies, mandating what risks to themselves individuals may or may not incur entails a form of paternalism that will often be required to meet especially demanding standards of justification.[477] If justified in the vehicle design context, why not similar constraints on potentially self-destructive risk-taking in many other contexts – smoking, consumption of alcohol or non-nutritious foods, motorcycle riding, hang-gliding, hunting, wilderness canoeing, and so on?

Fourth, while the Brookings study may have illuminated the impact of safety regulation on fatality rates, it does not provide a comprehensive explanation of the secular decline in fatality rates in most industrializing countries since the beginning of this century (sometimes referred to as 'Smeed's law').[478] More comparative empirical research would seem an important priority. What motivates 'Smeed's law' is far from clear. One could conjecture a learning-curve effect with increased exposure to risk,[479] but this provides no explanation of the factors that shape tastes for risk (or target levels of risk) or why they vary from one society to the next, or within one society over time. On the extreme risk homeostasis theory, as drivers become more skilled at handling one class of risks, one might have supposed that they are likely to take others, but then it is difficult to see why fatality rates would decline at all over time, unless a further theory is advanced to explain shifting tastes for, or target levels of, risk.

Indeed, Adams argues that general accident and violent fatality rates (from all causes) in most countries have remained remarkably constant over time, implying substitution effects among risky activities: 'If motorcycles were to be banned, young men would find other outlets for their risk taking proclivities – they might range from sky-diving to glue sniffing.'[480] Peltzman's own study fails to provide any convincing explanation of the dramatic, secular declines in fatality rates (which he freely accepts have occurred), although other studies, like the Brookings one, which take a much more optimistic view of safety regulation, offer little more by way of explanation. Indeed, Peltzman himself, in acknowledging that pre-regulation trends in fatality rates may partly reflect changes in highway design (more multi-lane highways),[481] seems to accept that not all safety improvements will be consumed as performance benefits, but when this will or will not occur is never precisely articulated.

8
Highway Safety Design

Introduction

The design of highway systems obviously entails a complex mix of objectives. Historically, traffic engineers have seen as their first priority designing highway features that produce and maintain a smooth flow of traffic so that highway systems can move as large a volume of traffic as possible as quickly as possible.[482] Over the last two decades or so, much more attention has been paid to safety features of highway design. This appears to parallel the increased focus on vehicle design and to reflect the influence of views such as those of Haddon,[483] who maintained that historically public policy has been excessively preoccupied with attempts to influence driver behaviour. The epidemiological approach took driver behaviour for the most part as given and designed vehicles and highways on the assumption that a significant proportion of driver error is irreducible or that a significant number of accidents are not in fact the product of driver error at all.

Obviously myriad features of highway design and maintenance may affect highway safety – road surface, road width, gradient, radius of curves, number of lanes, turning lanes, median strips, width of shoulder, run-off barriers, lighting, signs, stop-lights, stop signs, and so on. Within each of these categories of measures, substantial variations exist as to possible treatments of a given highway segment – for example, two- or four-way stop signs, traffic lights with or without pedestrian lights, rapid or slow amber lights, median strips with high 'forgiveness' and low penetration levels (or the converse). More than fifty highway design elements have been identified as having some type of safety relationship.[484]

These kinds of relationships are, of course, very general and provide little indication of precise design treatments for a given context. While many of the observations that follow are particularly pertinent to potential safety improvements in existing highway systems, there continue to be substantial amounts of new roadway construction, particularly in urban subdivision development, where designing road systems appropriately from the outset from a safety perspective is clearly preferable to correcting design errors subsequently, often at much greater cost.

In a trenchant critique of road safety design – both the established road system and additions to it – Hauer argues that its history has been characterized by 'a reign of ignorance.'[485] Hauer is highly critical of traffic engineers' tendency to follow established official manual guidelines uncritically and to avoid independent (non-self-interested) empirical evaluations of particular safety treatments, thus avoiding the risk that present practices may have to be radically changed and the existing stock of highways suddenly declared substandard.

According to Hauer, manual guidelines are commonly drawn up by committees of government officials and have typically been based on folklore rather than on scientifically based knowledge of safety implications of particular design variables. Where empirical evaluations of such variables have been undertaken, often far from robust and consistent findings have been forthcoming.[486] For example, Hauer reports that in 1982, the US Congress asked the National Academy of Science to study the safety cost-effectiveness of geometric design standards to be used in the rehabilitation of highways:

> A Committee was set up. To assist it, several experts in the field were hired to review what is known about the relationship between safety and some key highway features. The answers sought by the Committee were not for minutiae of design but for such basic questions as: how many accidents are saved by widening narrow lanes or shoulders, how many by reconstructing a sharp curve or by making the sight distances on a crest longer. The Committee was led to conclude that, 'Despite the widely acknowledged importance of safety in highway design, the scientific and engineering research necessary to answer these questions (i.e. about the relationship between roadway geometry and safety) is quite limited, sometimes contradictory and often insufficient to establish firm and scientifically defensible relationships.' (Transportation Research Board, 1987, p. 76). Coming after half a century of modern road building, this is an alarming finding.[487]

Just as important, findings that indicate a positive relationship between safety and particular highway improvements do not account for the costs of these improvements. Given a limited budget available for expenditures on highway improvements, it is obvious that not all improvements that may reduce accident rates can be undertaken. Choices must be made; a system of priorities must be established. While in Ontario little weight seems to be placed on formal techniques for determining a ranking of highway safety improvements, and reliance is placed mainly on the judgment and personal experience of traffic engineers, in the United States availability of federal funds to states for highway improvement (the 3 R program – resurfacing, restoration, and rehabilitation), beginning in the mid-1970s, has prompted attempts to refine in a more formal way the allocation process.[488] Although it is obviously not the purpose of this study to evaluate the costs and benefits of all possible alternative safety design features in all possible highway settings, it may be useful to comment briefly on part of the methodology that has emerged, and problems it confronts, for addressing the allocation problem.

Refining Allocation

Problem Identification

Obviously the first step in deciding whether an actual or potential accident site is a problem warranting high-priority attention is some definition of what constitutes 'a problem.' Particularly in urban areas, local residents may well view a single accident, for example, to a child in the neighbourhood, as defining an intersection or a cross-walk as a problem and mount political pressure for a safety intervention. Studies suggest that local political considerations often explain highway safety measures (traffic lights, one-way streets) in urban communities, even though more detached analysis may not be able to sustain the expenditures and indirect costs involved relative to other safety expenditures elsewhere in the highway system.[489]

Assuming, however, that these local political pressures can be resisted, or that with respect to large segments of the highway system (e.g. rural freeways) such pressures are not nearly as intense, a systematic approach to ranking safety improvement projects now finds favour in a number of US states. It involves collecting (and computerizing) accident reports from across the state highway system, noting configurations and causes of accidents and precise locations. An abnormally high level of accidents in a given location would trigger scrutiny. Merely counting accidents is likely to turn up mostly high-density areas of highway, relative to lightly travelled stretches of highway. Obviously, 'abnormally high' must be defined relative to some index in order to be meaningful. Typically, the index will be accidents per 100 million vehicle miles or, in the case of intersections, per million entering vehicles, across the state highway system, to which a similarly defined accident rate in the location in question can be compared.[490]

This so-called black spot approach to location identification sets priorities solely by reference to relative accident rates, thus ignoring relative costs of reducing accident rates in different locations. In addition, the abnormally high level of accidents in the period under scrutiny may be largely a random event or be explained by transitory factors (such as weather or construction in the area) and not carry any long-term significance.

Choice of Solution

These difficulties in problem identification aside, a formal approach to the choice of optimal solution to the problem is likely to involve some form of cost-benefit analysis. This form of analysis engenders various kinds of controversies and difficulties. Some analysts argue that one should employ such analysis not to identify safety 'needs' or to decide whether a response of some kind is appropriate, but only to determine the most effective type of response (cost-effectiveness, not cost-benefit analysis).[491] Other analysts, in theory at least, would wish to apply cost-benefit analysis to all proposed safety improvements to determine whether marginal benefits exceed marginal costs: investments in safety improvements should be made so as to maximize their net present worth or value (expected benefits minus expected costs discounted to present values).[492]

Even if this approach is accepted in principle, formidable difficulties remain to be resolved if it is to be operationalized in a reliable and acceptable way. First, valuing benefits from safety improvements necessarily entails placing monetary values on intangibles like life and limb. Much room for debate exists as to both how such valuations should be arrived at and, more fundamentally, whether such an explicit valuation exercise is ethically defensible at all. Cost-effectiveness analysis may be able to avoid such valuations by asking how, for a given budget, the most lives can be saved or personal injuries avoided, without comparing the total costs and benefits. In a cost-benefit framework, other gains from safety improvements (depending on their nature) should also in theory be taken account of – for example, increased capacity and operating speeds, reduced travel times, fuel savings, reduced air-pollution – although they will often be difficult to estimate. The direct costs of alternative safety improvements are typically much easier to estimate, although indirect costs (depending on the nature of the improvements) may be more difficult to estimate: for example, increased fuel consumption, pollution, driver delay, aesthetic detriment. Cost-benefit analysis is thus a very imprecise guide to policy making: indirect benefits and costs are often ignored because of estimation problems, and the intangible and subjective nature of the principal benefits entails rather arbitrary assignments of values. However, assuming that these issues (especially the latter) are treated consistently in comparing possible safety solutions, the analysis retains significant utility.

A different limitation on the utility of cost-benefit analysis is the partial context in which it is typically employed – the choice of optimal solution to a given, 'high-priority' problem (e.g. an identified 'black spot'). Ideally, all possible safety improvements in the entire traffic safety system should be simultaneously evaluated to determine how a predetermined budget for safety improvements can be invested so as to maximize the net present value of the resources to be invested. Perhaps, for example, in this more general or system-wide analysis, a large number of small improvements across the system would generate a higher net present value. These options seem unlikely to be revealed by the partial analysis of choice of solution to a pre-identified 'high-priority' problem. But this kind of system-wide analysis is scarcely feasible every time a budgetary allocation must be made, or perhaps ever, given the formidable information demands that it implies.

Evaluation

In an ideal allocation process, ex ante estimates of costs and benefits should be informed by prior experience with similar interventions and should be validated by subsequent assessments of the actual impact of the solution chosen in the case at hand, so that estimates of effects in future cases may be revised appropriately.

A number of methodological problems have been encountered in evaluation studies and partly account for widely divergent assessments of the impact of particular types of countermeasure.

Regression to the Mean in Time Series Studies: Hauer has pointed out that many time series ('before and after,' or 'event' studies) tend to overestimate the impact of particular safety improvement because of regression to the mean.[493] For example, if twenty fatalities occur at an intersection in a particular time period, leading to the installation of stop-lights, a reduction in fatalities to ten in the next time period may be attributed to the stop-lights when in fact the mean number of fatalities at the intersection over a substantial number of prior time periods may have only been ten. In other words, the post–safety improvement reduction in fatalities may simply be a regression to the prior mean, and the increase in fatalities prior to the safety improvement may have been simply a random event. The politics of highway safety interventions, especially in urban areas (noted above), may often reinforce this illusion of improvements. Unfortunately, errors may be perpetuated or extended as illusionary safety gains become the basis for generalized road design guidelines or warrants that traffic engineers subsequently rely on in 'treating' other accident sites.

Obviously, this methodological bias is soluble by taking sufficiently long before-and-after time periods so that random events do not unduly distort effects, although new problems may be generated by the intrusion of extraneous influences that may affect accident rates over longer periods. Alternatively, untreated 'control' settings can be used as reference points against which to measure the effects of interventions in similar settings.

Selection Bias in Cross-Sectional Studies: Cross-sectional studies that compare accident rates at various sites that are subject to different counter-measures and that are designed to evaluate the relative effectiveness of these different measures may yield distorted results if prior conditions, including accident rates, at each site are not adequately accounted for (as time-series studies attempt to do).[494] For example, in comparing the effectiveness of four-way with two-way stop signs, while accident rates in the former case may prove higher than in the latter, this may not imply lesser effectiveness of the former but rather the more severe nature of the problem that led to the installation of four-way stop signs in the first place (and which they may have significantly ameliorated). Again, careful methodology may be able to standardize for conditions at the various treatment sites under evaluation, although standardizing or adjusting for all relevant differences may be a complex task.

Accident Migration: In evaluating the impact of a counter-measure on the accident rate at a particular treatment site, it may be important to take account of countervailing effects elsewhere in the highway system. For example, Ebbecke and Shuster found that while the conversion of two-way to four-way stop signs in Philadelphia led to a 50 per cent reduction in accidents at intersections controlled by four-way stop signs, the accident rate at other intersections in the area under study increased correspondingly.[495]

Wright and Boyle,[496] in a study of 'black spot' treatment in London, estimated that accident frequency decreased at treated 'black spots' by 22.3 per cent but increased by 10 per cent in immediately adjacent links and nodes and may well have resulted in additional accidents in a larger surrounding area. The authors suggest that when accidents are avoided at the newly controlled intersection, so are many close calls. Drivers who had previously left the intersection shaken at a close call and driving more cautiously now drive less cautiously at neighbouring intersections.

Smith and Lovegrove[497] examined driver behaviour at two intersections, at the first of which was installed a stop sign. Using approach speed as an indicator of risk taking and accident potential, they concluded that the behaviour of infrequent commuters suggested that they compensated for the stop sign by increasing their speed but that regular commuters did not – that is, that some infrequent commuters were lulled into a false sense of security by the controlled intersection and were not prepared for the second, but that regular commuters, who knew the risks of the second intersection, gained the safety benefits of the first without sacrificing them on the second.

Risk Compensation More Generally

Adams, unsurprisingly, seizes the studies suggesting accident migration effects and other data to support his hypothesis of risk homeostasis, or at least substantial risk compensation.[498]

However, both Wright and Boyle's and Smith and Lovegrove's studies found substantial residual safety effects after risk compensation effects were subtracted. The suggestion in the former study that greater risk compensation effects may have been uncovered in a wider geographic search, while hypothetically possible, poses a non-falsifiable tautology – the effects, by hypothesis, are out there if only the universe is searched thoroughly enough for them.

Other evidence offered by Adams for risk homeostasis or an extreme risk compensation hypothesis with respect to highway improvements relates to the numbers of monthly highway fatalities and injuries in Ontario, which reflects lows in February, when road conditions are bad, and highs in August, when road conditions are good.[499] Adams argues that these data demonstrate that people take fewer risks in bad road conditions, in order to compensate for these conditions, but increase risk taking when road conditions are good, thus offsetting the better road conditions.[500] This inference seems highly suspect: the data provide not fatality or injury rates (i.e. per vehicle mile) but rather aggregate fatalities and injuries. Obviously people drive in Ontario much more in summer than in winter – July and August are peak vacation time.

What we need to know is the relative fatality and injury rates in, for example, February and August. Unless these are taken account of, it is impossible, on the risk homeostasis hypothesis, to explain a huge increase in target levels of risk from February to August. The hypothesis would rather imply that fatality and injury rates would remain constant over the year. If this were found to be so, the hypothesis would be strengthened but not conclusively proved, as the mix of rural and urban driving is likely also to change over these periods (and fatality rates have historically been higher on rural roads than on urban roads).

Adams acknowledges that fatality rates on limited-access motorways have been found to be much lower than on other roads but suggests that motorways have simply diverted longer-distance inter-city traffic from safer railway transportation to highway transportation and fostered the growth of traffic in the tributary parts of the road network that remain unimproved and where accident rates are higher.[501] In support of this view, he also cites the comparative US and British experience: 'The United States has enjoyed a very large lead over the rest of the world in vehicle ownership. A large proportion of its built environment was designed for the car. By contrast Britain has smaller cars and higher speed limits, and a much larger proportion of its road system predates mass car ownership. Yet Britain's road safety record is superior to that of the United States, judged either by deaths per 100,000 population, deaths per vehicle or by their respective positions relative to the Smeed Curve.'[502]

This comparison again seems highly suspect. While the death rate per 100,000 population in England was 11 in 1980, compared to 23 in the United States, the death rate per 1,000 vehicles was 0.30 in England, compared to 0.33 in the United States,[503] suggesting that many fewer people own or drive cars in England than in the United States and, more important, that those who do drive probably drive shorter distances. In other words, fatality rates per vehicle mile are required, at a minimum, in order for the British–American comparison to possess any utility. Where fatality rates for vehicle mile have been used in more careful assessments, such as the detailed multivariate study by Crandall et al.,[504] limited-access highways have been found significantly to reduce overall fatality rates.

Finally, if vehicle safety regulation and highway safety improvements are ruled out as contributors to the dramatic secular decline in fatality rates in many industrialized countries (of the order of 3–4 per cent a year on average over forty years), this places a specially strong burden on proponents of the risk homeostasis hypothesis, like Adams, to offer convincing alternative explanations. To date, this burden remains undischarged.

9
Post-Accident Injury Care

The final step in traffic safety counter-measures occurs after every other step has failed: the vehicle design did not avoid, or insulate the occupant from the impact of, the crash; the road design did not accommodate the error; and the driver failed to avoid it. Yet, even at that point, there is still room for intervention as emergency care and rehabilitation may mitigate the consequences of the accident.[505] There are two stages in post-crash care. The first deals with immediate emergency services. The second deals with long-term rehabilitation of disabled accident victims.

Emergency Care

The first and obvious point in emergency care is that faster is better. Two questions remain once the general result has been predicted. How much more can fatality rates be lowered through improved trauma care? And is it worth the money spent? With respect to this latter question, there has been little attempt made to assess whether the costs entailed in special trauma services justify the benefits, and some distaste for engaging explicitly in such an analysis. However, some estimates claim that if the United States were to establish a system of trauma centres similar to that which

West Germany has set up along its main autobahns since the early 1970s, over the first year the US GNP would be increased by more than $2 billion and additional taxes paid would amount to more than $550 million.[506]

The acceptance of emergency treatment as a large-scale project for the lowering of fatalities resulting from trauma has a long military history dating back to Greek and Roman times. In more modern times, experience with 'flying hospitals' in the Napoleonic Wars, field stations in the First and Second World Wars, mobile surgical hospitals in the Korean War, and corps surgical hospitals in the Vietnam War all showed that reducing the time between injury and definitive surgical treatment dramatically reduces mortality rates.[507] The introduction of the helicopter for transporting wounded relocated the scene of trauma care from the field to the hospital.[508]

These experiences have also influenced treatment of accident victims and redirected attention away from first-aid to trauma centres and rapid transportation of the victim to these centres. The expression used by trauma-care personnel is 'The Golden Hour,' referring to the critical one-hour period following injury. If an accident victim can be transported to a hospital or trauma centre within that time, chances of survival are considered excellent.

In 1961, F.H. Van Wagoner performed a three-year study of fatal accidents that proceeded from trauma.[509] Van Wagoner examined autopsy reports to determine whether any of the deaths were salvageable. He concluded that 33 per cent of those who died could have been saved by better trauma care. This article is often cited as a break-through in evaluation of trauma care,[510] and Van Wagoner's method has been used as the basis for an extensive subsequent literature on trauma evaluation.

The surprising feature of subsequent studies is that there appears to be no general downward trend in preventable deaths through the years. Studies continue to find on average that the incidence of preventable deaths resulting from inadequate trauma care varies between 30 and 40 per cent.[511] Perhaps as methods of emergency care have improved, expectations of the evaluators increase and a non-preventable death is now classified as a preventable death.

Gains are more obvious in studies of discrete trauma care interventions. For example, in San Diego County, California, a study[512] revealed that 13.6 per cent of fatalities were preventable and that treatment of major trauma victims was sub-optimal in 32 per cent of cases. After introduction of a trauma system in the county, a check was done by the same audit group. The preventable death rate dropped to 2.7 per cent and sub-optimal care was found in only 4.2 per cent of cases. Another study recently completed in Orange County, California, found that the preventable death category fell from 73 per cent to 4 per cent when patients were taken to a trauma centre rather than a conventional hospital.[513]

Another explanation for the modest aggregate decline in preventable deaths from trauma is insufficient investment in a system of specialized trauma centres with surgical teams on call on a twenty-four hour basis. The West German system is often held out as a model. There are now thirty-two air-rescue stations in the country, as well as ground transportation systems, and it is estimated that 90 per cent of the population is within fifteen minutes of a trauma centre.[514]

Rehabilitation

Rehabilitation, including physical, vocational, and emotional rehabilitation, is the second aspect of post-crash care strategies. Rehabilitation attempts to restore the victim as closely as possible to the quality of life-style enjoyed before the accident. A comprehensive and critical review of the literature on rehabilitation is beyond our scope here; the relevant literature is not simply a subcategory of traffic safety research but a larger scientific and medical field of specialty that addresses many different sources of disablement.

Two issues, however, warrant brief comment: the value of investment in rehabilitation and the form of compensation scheme most conducive to rehabilitation.

In the US Department of Transportation's 1985 analysis of no-fault insurance systems,[515] findings on the costs and benefits of rehabilitation are reviewed. The department relies principally on a survey by the property and casualty insurance industry's All-Industry Research Advisory Council (AIRAC) of 404 seriously injured auto accident victims in the unlimited medical benefit states of Michigan, Pennsylvania, and New Jersey. The first finding indicates how expensive rehabilitation can often be. Lifetime treatment of the 357 claimants receiving rehabilitation was expected to cost a total of $438,900 on average. Lifetime treatment of the 51 claimants who did not attempt any rehabilitation was expected to cost a total of $211,700 on average. A follow-up survey four years later showed that of those victims attempting rehabilitation 86 per cent showed much or some improvement. The expected total payments for the 33 per cent of victims who showed 'much' improvement was far less (279,400) than the expected total payments for individuals who failed to improve at all as a result of rehabilitation ($554,000) or who showed only some improvement ($512,400). Average total payments expected to be made for each victim currently employed was $304,500, whereas those for each victim who was unemployed and currently unemployable was $674,000. Rehabilitation can dramatically increase the prospects of employment: 65 per cent of the people who underwent vocational rehabilitation at Chicago's Rehabilitation Institute between 1978 and 1980 were placed in productive employment. The Insurance Bureau of Michigan, in its 1978 review of no-fault auto insurance in that state, claimed that 'recent estimates have shown that for every dollar spent on rehabilitation $9 are returned through increased productivity.'[516]

Two observations are perhaps warranted. First, for seriously injured accident victims, rehabilitation is likely to be very expensive. Second, it is likely to achieve substantial improvements in only a minority of cases. Obviously, in those cases, the substantial expenditures are likely to be worthwhile. Again, it is commonly argued that governments have insufficiently invested in the provision of appropriate rehabilitation facilities that fully address physical, vocational, and emotional needs.[517]

The issue of the choice of a compensation plan as it relates to rehabilitation is part of a wider debate concerning the optimal auto insurance compensation scheme. It is often argued that two criteria are required in a compensation scheme to promote rehabilitation: speed of payment, in order to allow therapy to be commenced quickly, which apparently greatly enhances effectiveness; and provision of an emotional environment conducive to rehabilitation. According to critics of the tort liability–based system, the present system fails on both counts.

The delay in payment may be years in a serious injury case and months even in a minor one.[518] The establishment of first-party, no-fault benefits, in theory, addresses the problem of interim payments needed for the start of therapy. The US Department of Transportation's recent study of US no-fault schemes finds that compensation flows much more quickly to victims under no-fault schemes than traditional tort third-party insurance schemes and in this respect is much more conducive to rehabilitation.[519]

Next to delay, the very orientation of fault-based compensation systems is claimed to frustrate attempts at rehabilitation.[520] Although some blame the problem on the adversarial nature of the process, Ison argues that the problem lies in the combination of an aetiological focus on the cause of the injuries with the adversarial system.[521] The success of rehabilitation rests on the patient being determined to overcome the disability, to forget the injury, and to look forward.

The present tort liability system forces the victim to look back, because in order to receive any compensation the disability must have been caused by the car accident. Moreover, the quantum of compensation substantially turns on being able to demonstrate to a judge or jury the extensiveness of physical, economic, and emotional losses that resulted. For example, Dooley found in an empirical study both that patients involved in ongoing litigation had more perceived disability and that 'compensation patients evidenced much greater difficulties maintaining improvement or returning to productive activity.'[522]

Everything in the fault system – its aetiological basis, its adversarial nature, its delays, its uncertainties – is claimed to retard and frustrate rehabilitation.

Conclusion

This survey of techniques for controlling traffic accidents reveals much greater inconclusiveness and uncertainty than we had expected to find when we embarked upon the study. We had hoped to be able to discover what interventions worked or did not work and be able to apply this knowledge to other areas of conduct where public policy experience has been less long-standing and intensive. Vast social resources have been devoted to various traffic safety measures and a formidable body of multidisciplinary research has developed. Despite this experience, very little can be said with confidence about the effectiveness of alternative counter-measures.

One explanation for this deep ambiguity seems to reside in the inherently multicausal nature of accidents. Accidents are products of myriad necessary and often interactive conditions. Determining what conditions, if changed, are likely to reduce the frequency or severity of accidents has proved daunting and frustrating. As lawyers trained to focus on the primary proximate cause of accidents and other harms, we have had to adjust our perspective to take account of the epidemiological insight that changes in any of a variety of necessary and interactive conditions may reduce the frequency and severity of accidents.

Standard research methodology in evaluating the effect of particular counter-measures has typically entailed time-series, cross-sectional, or cross-jurisdictional analysis, but the host of confounding variables that are typically operative at any one time have often engendered severe difficulties in isolating the effects of a particular counter-measure from all the surrounding influences. As a result, robust and uncontroversial inferences as to the effects of any particular counter-measures have rarely been sustainable.

Fortunately, there has been a broadening of methods used in recent traffic research. Econometric modelling, for example, can provide insights into the range of factors influencing accidents. Other studies have tried to assess the range of socio-cultural factors that may also influence accidents. Comparisons among different jurisdictions, some of which have experienced changes in policy or practice, can shed light on the utility of various counter-measures. True experiments, however, where different policies are applied to one group of drivers relative to a control group, have rarely been undertaken, in part because courts and enforcement officials have not seen themselves as appropriate vehicles for experimental research and in part because of ethical and political sensitivities to exposing subgroups of drivers to contrived differentials in risk exposures or penalty levels.

In addition, fragmentation in responsibility for formulation and enforcement of different aspects of traffic safety policy among three levels of government (federal, provincial, and municipal) and further fragmentation of responsibility among agencies within any given level of government (e.g. highways and policing) have severely inhibited development of a unifying evaluative perspective on the relative effectiveness of the wide range of counter-measures for which these different levels and agencies of government assume responsibility.

Along with the political, bureaucratic, and regulatory incentives that each class of public-sector actor has in order to maintain the importance of the counter-measures for which it is responsible, private-sector interest groups have strong incentives to promote or oppose particular kinds of counter-measures, whatever the long-term safety effects of the policies espoused. For example, the highway construction industry no doubt finds it in its interests to emphasize highway design improvements; the automobile manufacturing industry, to oppose cost-increasing, and hence demand-reducing, vehicle safety design improvements. The liquor and hospitality industries and young people find it in their interests to oppose increases in the drinking age; the auto industry and youthful drivers, to oppose increases in the driving age. Bereaved parents who have lost children at the hands of drunk drivers are unlikely to be assuaged by technological responses to the drunk driving problem and will demand retribution from deviant drivers through more severe criminal sanctions. Libertarian and other interests will oppose devices and investigative techniques that restrict freedom of choice and mobility.[523] Thus, system-wide use of cost-benefit or cost-effectiveness analysis has been accorded very limited weight in evaluating the relative effectiveness of alternative traffic safety counter-measures. Comprehensive long-term planning is difficult when one is reacting to short-term pressures and entrenched interests.

The evidence reviewed in this study suggests practical and ethical limits on the extent to which the criminal law can be used to affect behaviour. No doubt massive and sustained surveillance and prosecutions can raise seat-belt use to very high levels, can keep most speeders under control, and can eliminate much drinking and driving. But this requires an enormous cost in terms of police, prosecutorial, and court resources as well as constant intrusive observations of citizens' behaviour. And many of the drivers with the poorest safety records will be the last to buckle up and will continue to speed and to drink and drive. The criminal process has increasing difficulty in affecting the conduct of higher-risk groups of drivers. Keeping enforcement levels moderate but increasing penalties can create problems, such as lack of willingness to prosecute, inclination to defend vigorously, court congestion, increased plea bargaining, prison overcrowding, and other distortion effects. Severe penalties will be seen by many as being unfair in relation to conduct involved. Community support for traffic safety enforcement and law enforcement in general may diminish if penalties are perceived as too severe in relation to sanctioned conduct or if enforcement techniques unduly restrict mobility or intrude on privacy. This simply raises the larger point that there are real limits on how much society is willing to pay for traffic safety.

We are not suggesting that laws and the criminal process are not important in controlling traffic flow and traffic accidents. The mere existence of a mandatory seat-belt law, for example, will increase the level of use. Enforcement will also increase use further. Most people will comply with a law without weighing the advantages or disadvantages of doing so. Moreover, the use of criminal sanctions shows that the state is concerned about the conduct and, as in the case of drinking and driving, serves an important moralizing, socializing, habit-forming, and educational function beyond simply increasing the formal costs of non-conforming behaviour. To some extent, civil liability will also have the same effect. We do not yet know enough about the use of the criminal and civil law in establishing norms in the community. This is a fruitful area for further research by many disciplines.

But even if the criminal law can effectively control conduct, the important question is whether this will affect accidents. Studies of accident rates during police slowdowns and of the relationship between drunk-driving arrests and alcohol-related accidents cast doubt on the connection between targeted conduct and accidents. Policy-makers sometimes forget that the object of policing is to reduce traffic accidents, not simply to sanction prohibited conduct.

The police tend to enforce the laws that are technological-ly easy to enforce. Speed limits can easily be enforced with radar, and drinking and driving with the breathalyser. Fixed limits, such as a speed limit of 100 km/h or 0.08 in the breathalyser, encourage police to concentrate much of their traffic resources on speed traps and drunk driving road-blocks, diverting resources from the more difficult to ap-prehend cases of demonstrated dangerous driving, such as the driver weaving from side to side or passing at high speeds from lane to lane or running red lights. The ease of apprehension and the success rate in terms of convictions are much higher for the routine case.

Tort liability can help in controlling traffic accidents, both by reducing exposure levels and by creating incentives to take care. Society has tended to depreciate its effectiveness. It can help to curtail the exposure of higher-risk categories of drivers by the pricing of insurance both for categories of drivers and for those with previous accidents or traffic viola-tions. Other techniques, such as experience rating and man-dating a compulsory deductible of a significant amount, which cannot be insured against by anyone suffering dam-age or being sued, would provide an additional incentive for drivers to take care.

With respect to traffic safety counter-measures that centre on use of rewards for responsible driving behaviour, we have noted that such strategies have not been widely used but that such evidence as exists suggests some promise in fuller use of reward-based strategies. However, in at least some contexts, there is likely to be societal resistance to rewarding all drivers who act responsibly (i.e. doing what good citizens should do anyway), rather than penalizing that subset of anti-social drivers who act irresponsibly. Some controlled experimentation, such as giving free licence rene-wals to a sample of those who have been accident-free for the past year, would be worth trying.

With respect to environmentally oriented traffic safety counter-measures, such as safer highway or vehicle design, the evidence is somewhat ambiguous. On balance one seems justified in inferring that improved vehicle design has significantly reduced auto-related fatalities and injuries, even after allowing for offsetting risk compensation effects. This is particularly true of seat-belts and airbags. Similarly, the secular decline in fatality rates seems at least in part attributable to improved highway design, including the increased percentage of limited-access, multi-lane highways in the road system.

However, even if these safety benefits can be demonstrated, little analysis has been undertaken to compare costs with benefits. Ideally, for such analysis to be effective, vehicle and highway design improvements need to be disaggregated into particular design features, and a two-stage analysis undertaken: first, of whether the net present value of the particular measure is positive and, second, of whether a higher net present value might be realized from alternative counter-measures not only in the particular policy context under consideration but anywhere else across the entire traffic safety system.

Apart from the formidable and perhaps unattainable information requirements that such a rigorous form of cost-benefit analysis implies, the existing institutional fragmentation of public-sector responsibilities in traffic safety administration severely inhibits its adoption. Perhaps centralization of licensing, sanctioning, highway construction, and auto design, along with health care, would give us a more unified perspective. However, in the absence of some such approach, costs per life saved or injury avoided are likely to vary dramatically from one counter-measure to another across the system, implying that major reallocations of resources could generate vastly better total pay-offs from total investments in traffic safety.[524]

Setting these difficulties aside, a distributional difficulty arises with environmentally oriented counter-measures, even assuming that their net impact is positive. Moving from driver-centred seat-belt usage requirements to the more expensive compulsory passive restraints will mean that drivers who currently buckle up will be cross-subsidizing those who do not. More generally, less risky drivers will cross-subsidize more risky drivers. As the price decreases, however, imposition of this cross-subsidization becomes easier to justify. One of the prime beneficiaries of passive restraints is a publicly funded health care system, and perhaps public funds should in part be used to subsidize the cost of these systems.

This tension between individual responsibility and collective interests is present in many of the traffic safety issues in this study. Individual responsibility is often ineffective, but collective responsibility is by its very nature overinclusive. Political resolution of this strong tension between competing philosophical viewpoints often takes precedence over scientific study of the effectiveness of various techniques.

One class of intervention that emerges from our survey as exhibiting significantly positive traffic safety effects is exposure-limiting counter-measures. This class of counter-measure is underemphasized in the original Haddon matrix, where it is subsumed into all interventions that target drivers' behaviour in the pre-crash phase. However, unlike other such interventions, exposure-restricting counter-measures seek primarily not to change driver behaviour on the highway but rather to exclude identified classes of high-risk drivers from the highway. Empirical evidence suggests fairly unambiguously that measures such as increasing the drinking age; increasing the driving age; increasing the pricing of alcohol or fuel; imposing night-time curfews on young drivers; confronting high-risk classes of drivers with higher insurance premiums, thereby pricing some of them off the road; and imposing licence suspensions on severely deviant drivers significantly reduce fatality and accident rates.

At one level, of course, the effectiveness of exposure-limiting counter-measures is intuitively obvious – the one certain way of reducing traffic accidents to zero is by excluding everyone from the roads. We would all, of course, recognize that the costs of such an overinclusive counter-measure would vastly outweigh the benefits. The question that more finely targeted exposure-restricting counter-measures raises is similar: even if targeted on putatively high-risk classes of drivers, will the costs outweigh what appear to be convincingly demonstrated safety benefits?

The costs of exposure-reducing counter-measures are significant. Exposure-limiting interventions directed at high-risk drivers such as teenagers or drivers with high demerit and accident levels target only a small percentage of the population at risk. Moreover, they are overinclusive: aggregate behaviour of the group and past events such as traffic convictions or accidents are not particularly strong predictors of probabilistic future events such as accidents, which are the product of many interactive conditions. To the extent that young drivers' disproportionate accident risk is a factor of their inexperience with driving, exposure-limiting counter-measures may engender significant offsetting effects when older drivers begin to drive.

Classification for exposure-limiting measures on the basis of age, gender, or socio-economic factors is often considered unfair if done by state actors, but perhaps not if done by insurance companies. Evidence suggests that those subject to exposure-reduction measures often continue to drive, but less frequently and more cautiously. This more cautious, though illegal driving might produce habit-forming, more careful driving in the future. Exposure reduction is achieved through the threat of formal sanctions if the prohibitions on driving are violated; yet exposure reduction often operates as a compliance technique in changing behaviour in ways not spelled out in the law and without initial reliance on prosecutions.

One particular compliance technique that we believe could be more effectively used for traffic safety purposes is the licensing system. Licensing can be used, for example, to restrict the driving of young drivers and help them to gain experience in the least hazardous ways possible, and licence suspensions can be more finely tuned to permit some driving under controlled conditions. Despite the significant costs that accompany their use, we remain optimistic about the relative potential of exposure-reducing techniques.

We note that, in general, exposure-reducing techniques are implemented through methods of regulation and surveillance designed to achieve compliance without initially relying on the obtaining of convictions through the police and court systems. Compliance techniques in the area of drinking and driving can, for example, enlist the aid of licensed servers of alcohol, the alcohol industry, insurance companies, and friends or parents, without placing exclusive reliance on the proactive policing that typifies enforcement of sanctions in the traffic field.

It is instructive to think about the comparative treatment of cars and guns in Canada and the United States. There has been and is very little difference between the experience of Canada and the United States in relation to cars and road safety. Ownership, exposure, road conditions, and car safety are not dissimilar from one side of the border to another. Not surprisingly, as we saw in the introduction, vehicle accident rates are also not dissimilar.

In contrast, however, comparison of handgun deaths from one country to the other shows a remarkably different picture.[525] Instead of the death rate being the same, the American death rate per capita is twenty times as high as in Canada. In 1979 there were fewer than sixty homicides committed with handguns in all of Canada. In the same year there were over 10,000 handgun homicides in the United States. For over 100 years Canada has carefully controlled the use of handguns, through a system of registration certificates and permits, under strong federal laws and administration. Rather than dealing with the use of handguns through criminal prosecutions after their improper use, Canada regulated and controlled their use in advance, through a licensing system. No doubt the traditional Canadian deference to authority and centralization of authority over criminal law in the federal government facilitated passage of these laws, just as they may have assisted in introduction of compulsory seat-belt legislation ten years before similar laws in the United States. And the absence of handgun manufacturers in Canada eliminated a powerful pressure group. Nevertheless, the difference between the treatment of cars and that of guns in the two countries is striking and suggests that compliance-based licensing systems may become more effective in preventing harm than deterrence-based prosecution systems.

We do not suggest that anywhere near the vigilance applicable to firearms should be applied to automobiles. We do, however, raise the question whether some of the licensing techniques that have controlled the exposure of high-risk handguns in Canada cannot be more widely used, albeit in a modified form, to control the exposure of high-risk, if not all drivers.

No one technique of control is the entire answer. Controlling exposure through licensing, for example, may well reduce the number of accidents, but there will still be a vast quantity remaining. Prosecutions, civil liability, rewards, highway design and maintenance, vehicle safety, and post-accident procedures all have some impact on the frequency and severity of traffic accidents. What we do not know, however, is where lies the greatest pay-off on the marginal dollar devoted to traffic safety. This is the central policy issue that traffic safety research has barely begun to confront.

NOTES

1 This study takes into account the Report of the Ontario Automobile Insurance Board, dated 14 July 1989, *Re an Examination of threshold no fault and choice no fault systems of privately delivered automobile insurance* (see note 326a, below), but does not cover the Ontario government's later no-fault bill.

2 An earlier volume, M.L. Friedland, ed., *Sanctions and Rewards in the Legal System: A Multidisciplinary Approach* (Toronto: University of Toronto Press, 1989), recently appeared, as did M.L. Friedland, ed., *Securing Compliance: Seven Case Studies* (Toronto: University of Toronto Press, 1990), in which the current work is chapter 4.

3 The Ontario data have been taken from the annual reports of the Ontario Ministry of Transportation and Communications and from *Estimates of Population for Canada and the Provinces* produced by Statistics Canada. The American data have been taken from the US Bureau of the Census *Statistical Abstract of the United States*. Some of these figures have been approximated, and all have been rounded. The figures cannot reflect a completely accurate picture because of changes in reporting criteria over the years.

4 Calculated using data from annual reports of the Department of Highways, Ontario, 1930 and 1931 (Toronto: King's Printer, 1932) 276; *Ontario Road Safety Annual Report* (Toronto: Ministry of Transportation and Communications, 1987) 8.

5 *Report of Inquiry into Motor Vehicle Accident Compensation in Ontario* (hereinafter Osborne Report) (Toronto: Queen's Printer, 1988) 739.

6 Dominion Bureau of Statistics, *Vital Statistics 1930* (Ottawa: King's

Printer, 1933) 194; Ministry of Transportation and Communications *Annual Report 1979–80* (Toronto: Ministry of Transportation and Communications 1980) 40; *Ontario Road Safety Annual Report* (Toronto: Ministry of Transportation and Communications, 1987) 8. The projection for Ontario for 1988 was 1,205, based on statistics for the first three months of 1988. The Canadian fatality statistics for 1987 were 4,285; Transport Canada's *1987 Canadian Motor Vehicle Traffic Accident Statistics.* The projection for 1988 based on the first six months of 1988 was 3,976 road fatalities in 1988: Transport Canada leaflet, February 1989.

7 Statistics Canada, *Vital Statistics: Causes of Death*; US Bureau of Census, *Statistical Abstract of the United States.* See also G.W. Trinca et al., *Reducing Traffic Injury: A Global Challenge* (Melbourne: Royal Australasian College of Surgeons, 1988) chapter 2, for statistics on traffic injuries in many countries; this important manuscript contains much thoughtful material on ways to control traffic accidents.

   Traffic deaths and injuries in the Soviet Union are very high. A Reuter's report from Moscow in the *Globe and Mail*, 9 February 1989, states: 'Deaths on Soviet roads last year were almost three times higher than total losses suffered by the Soviet army in more than nine years of combat in Afghanistan, the army daily Krasnaya Zvezda said yesterday. Major-General V.G. Ishutin told the newspaper in an interview that 47,072 people died in a total of 272,748 road accidents last year and 296,979 were injured. More than one-fifth of the crashes involved drunken drivers.'

   A separate Reuters report in the *Globe and Mail* the same day notes the relatively low number of persons killed in airplane crashes the same year: 'Eighty-five people were killed in 16 Soviet airplane crashes in 1988, officials of the state airline Aeroflot said yesterday. The death toll was much higher than a year before, when 18 people died in 13 crashes.'

8 Osborne Report 750; *Ontario Road Safety Annual Report* (Toronto: Ministry of Transportation and Communications, 1987) 8.

9 US Bureau of Census, *Statistical Abstract* (1971) 540, (1987) 588.

10 *OECD Road Safety Research: A Synthesis* (Paris: OECD, 1986) 13. The trend is sometimes referred to as 'Smeed's law' (after British transportation analyst R.J. Smeed, who first drew attention to such a phenomenon in 1949), which postulates declining fatality rates with increased industrialization and motorization. See J.G.U. Adams, *Risk*

and Freedom (Cardiff: Transport Publishing Projects, 1985); J.G.U. Adams, 'Smeed's Law, Seat Belts and the Emperor's New Clothes,' in L. Evans and R.C. Schwing, eds., *Human Behavior and Traffic Safety* (New York: Plenum Press, 1985).

11 *Ontario Road Safety Annual Report* (Toronto: Ministry of Transportation and Communications, 1987) 8.

12 Osborne Report, Vol. I, 742, Vol. II, 749ff. Estimates of economic costs of US motor vehicle accidents using various models and reporting criteria vary from $23.5 to 69 billion: see ibid., vol. II, 749; US Bureau of Census, *Statistical Abstracts of the United States* (1987) 107th ed. (Washington, DC) 588.

13 *Ontario Road Safety Annual Report* (Toronto: Ministry of Transportation and Communications, 1987) 8.

14 Ibid., 60.

15 Statistics Canada, *Juristat* 8 no. 4 (Ottawa: Minister of Supply and Services, September 1988). Highway Traffic Act convictions amount to about five times the charges laid for all Criminal Code offences, traffic and otherwise: Canadian Centre for Justice Statistics, *Canadian Crime Statistics 1985* (Ottawa: Ministry of Supply and Services Canada, 1986) 2–53.

16 Adopted from the Osborne Report, Vol. I, chapter 17.

17 Waller reports that the first traffic fatality in Britain occurred in 1898. The fatality was originally blamed on reckless and fast driving, but later the primary cause was found to be a wheel made of poorly seasoned wood. See J. Waller, *Inquiry Control* (Lexington: D.C. Heath, 1985) 107. Despite initial hopes that the automobile as a 'tamed animal' would be safer than the horse as a means of transportation, automobile accident rates and fatalities surpassed those of horse-drawn vehicles in the United States by approximately 1909: J. Eastman, *Styling versus Safety* (Lanham, Md: University Press of America, 1984) 14.

18 Offences Against the Person Act, 1861 (UK), 24–25 Vict., c. 100, s. 35; Criminal Code of Canada, 1892, 55–56 Vict., c. 29, s. 253 (taken from) RSC 1886, c. 162, s. 28, (taken from) Offences Against the Person Act, 1869, 32–33 Vict., c. 20, s. 34.

19 *Motor Car Act*, 1903 (UK), 3 Edw. 7, c. 36, s. 1; The Motor Vehicle Act, SO 1906, c. 46, s.7.

20 Public Highways in Upper Canada Act, 1855, 18 Vict., c. 138, s. 4; The Licensing Act, 1872 (UK) 35 & 36 Vict., c. 94, s. 12.

21 For drunk driving, see Criminal Code of Canada, SC 1921, c. 25, s. 3; for reckless driving, see Criminal Code Amendment, SC 1910, c. 13, s. 1.

22 A.J. Reiss, 'Consequences of Compliance and Deterrence Models of Law Enforcement for the Exercise of Police Discretion' (1984) 47 *Law and Contemporary Problems* 83 at 85.

23 Ibid., 94.

24 R. Borkenstein, 'Historical Perspective: North American Traditional and Experimental Response,' *Journal of Studies on Alcohol* Supp. 10 (July 1985) 3 at 4.

25 Eastman, *Styling versus Safety* 150–1.

26 Motor Car Act, 1903 (UK), 3 Edw. 7, c. 36, ss. 2–3; Motor Vehicles Act, SO (1903), c. 27, s. 4; J. Flink, *The Car Culture* (Cambridge, Mass: MIT Press, 1975) 26.

27 Eastman, *Styling versus Safety* 150. Proposals for pre-licensing testing of drivers' abilities or knowledge were rejected in Britain as 'either perfunctory or ineffective' and were not introduced until the 1930s: see *Report of the Royal Commission on Motor Cars* (1906) 27, paragraph 94; *Royal Commission on Transport, First Report* (1929) 28, paragraph 41; W. Plowden, *The Motor Car and Politics 1896–1970* (London: Bodley Head, 1971) 56.

28 Motor Vehicle Act, SO (1906), c. 46, s. 16.

29 W.A. Dinsdale, *History of Accident Insurance* (London: Stone & Cox, 1954) 177.

30 Barry Supple, *The Royal Exchange Assurance* (Cambridge: University Press, 1970) 233; W.A. Dinsdale, *History of Accident Insurance* (London: Stone & Cox, 1954) 45.

31 Shaw wrote: 'What is urgent – what you must have above all is insurance against "third party claims". If you get killed you are dead. If the car is smashed, *it* is dead. But if it runs into a motor bus or a beanfeast, everybody in it can take action against you, and even keep on taking actions against you until the end of their lives every time they have a fresh nervous symptom, and get enormous damages. You may have to support them and their children for ever. And you will have to buy a new bus for the company. Your salary will be attached; you will be reduced to beg on the streets. This always happens in the first 5 minutes with an uninsured car.' See A. Dent, ed., *Bernard Shaw and Mrs. Patrick Campbell: Their Correspondence* (London: Victor Gollancz, 1952) 133. Most motorists would not have

shared Shaw's flare for the dramatic, but they may well have been motivated by the incentives he portrays to obtain insurance.

32 Road Traffic Act (1930), 20 & 21 Geo. 5, c. 43, Part II.

33 James Foreman-Peck, 'Death on the Roads: Changing National Responses to Motor Accidents,' in T. Barker, ed., *The Economic and Social Effects of the Spread of Motor Vehicles* (London: MacMillan, 1987) 279ff.

34 Ibid., 282.

35 E. Tenney, *The Highway Jungle* (New York: Exposition Press, 1962) 90–1.

36 Locomotives on Highway Act, 1896 (UK), 50 & 60 Vict., c. 36, ss. 2–3; Motor Vehicles Act, SO (1903), c. 27, s. 5.

37 See, generally, Eastman, *Styling versus Safety.*

38 *Report on the Royal Commission on Motor Cars* (1906) 26, paragraph 91. Some safety advocates argued that 'speeding' was inevitable as long as cars had the mechanical capacity to exceed desired speed levels: see Eastman, *Styling versus Safety* 85–6.

39 *Report on the Royal Commission on Motor Cars* (1906) 18, paragraph 55; J. Flink, *The Car Culture* (Cambridge, Mass.: MIT Press, 1975) 175.

40 T.C. Willet, *Criminal on the Road* (London: Tavistock, 1964) 65–6.

41 See, generally, W. Plowden, *The Motor Car and Politics 1896–1970* (London: Bodley Head, 1971).

42 *Report of the Royal Commission on Motor Cars* (1906) 10, paragraph 2; *Royal Commission on Transport, First Report* (1929) 3, paragraph 3.

43 The first royal commission commented: 'We think that the object of the law should be not to punish speed because it is speed, but because and where it is dangerous or otherwise injurious to the public.' See *Report of the Royal Commission on Motor Cars* (1906) 10, paragraph 2.

44 *Royal Commission on Transport, First Report* (1929) 3, paragraph 5.

45 Road Traffic Act, 1930 (UK), 20 & 21 Geo. 5, c. 43, s. 10, and First Schedule therein; Road Traffic Act, 1934 (UK), 24 & 25 Geo. 5, c. 50, ss. 1, 2, and First Schedule therein.

46 Provisions for insurance to compensate those injured in automobile accidents and requirements that drivers stop and offer assistance after an accident were forms of legal interventions that regulated behaviour after an accident. See for example Motor Car Act, (1903) (UK), 3 Edw. 7, c. 36, s. 6; Motor Vehicle Act, SO 1906, c. 46, s. 11; Criminal Code Amendment, SC 1910, c. 13, s. 2.

47 Plowden, *The Motor Car* 284.

48 One researcher, writing in 1942, concluded: 'A major reduction in accidents inevitably depends on driver improvement ... if we apply the full resources of our intelligence, we can implant in drivers new and more suitable modes of behaviour'; H. DeSilva, *Why We Have Automobile Accidents* (New York: John Wiley, 1942) ix.

49 The pioneer in this field was Hugh De Haven, who became interested in design methods to lessen injuries after he had survived an air crash and witnessed an automobile accident in which a driver was disfigured after his head struck a sharp steel knob on the dashboard of the car. See, generally, Eastman, *Styling versus Safety* 209ff.

In 1952, physicist William Harper outlined the difference between approaches that emphasized reduction of accidents and those that attempted to reduce injuries and thus revealed the logic of the 'second collision.' He stated: 'It is strange, indeed, that safety belts were not used on cars from the very beginning. If brakes were considered logical mechanisms for cars, why was it that no one considered it advisable that they also be made available to the car occupants? Why stop the car if the occupants can't stop?'; W. Harper, 'Prevention and Reduction of Injuries in Traffic Collisions' (1952) 43 *Journal of Criminal Law, Criminology and Police Science* 515, at 525.

50 R. Nader, *Unsafe at Any Speed: The Designed-In Dangers of the American Automobile* (New York: Grossman, 1965); J. O'Connell and A. Myers, *Safety Last: An Indictment of the Auto Industry* (New York: Random House, 1966).

51 As early as 1959 Daniel Patrick Moynihan, then an academic, criticized traditional approaches to motor vehicle safety and championed a new focus on automobile design and reduction of injuries. Moynihan argued that 'admonishing individuals to drive carefully seems a little bit like trying to stop a typhoid epidemic by urging each family to boil its own drinking water and not eat oysters; that may help, of course, but why not try vaccinations, setting standards of cleanliness for food handlers and purifying *everybody's* drinking water in the reservoirs?'; D.P. Moynihan, 'Epidemic on the Highways,' *Reporter*, 30 April 1959, 16 at 17.

52 National Traffic and Motor Vehicle Safety Act, Pub. L. No. 89-563, 80 Stat. 718 (1967). See, generally, the excellent account provided by Jerry Mashaw and David Harfst in 'Regulation and Legal Culture: The Case of Motor Vehicle Safety' (1987) 4 *Yale Journal of Regulation*

257, and their forthcoming book *Regulating the Freedom Machine* (Harvard University Press).

53 W. Haddon, 'A Logical Framework for Categorizing Highway Safety Phenomena and Activity' (1972) 12 *Journal of Trauma* 193 at 196.

54 W. Haddon, jr, was named first director of the new National Highway Traffic Safety Administration, charged with administering the new legislation.

55 W. Haddon, 'Advances in the Epidemiology of Injuries as a Basis for Public Policy' (1980) 95 *Public Health Reports* 411 at 414.

56 W. Haddon and S. Baker, 'Injury Control,' in D. Clark and B. MacMahon, eds., *Preventive and Community Medicine* 2d ed. (Boston: Little Brown, 1981) 110.

57 Ibid., 111.

58 W. Haddon, 'On the Escape of Tigers: An Ecologic Note' (1970) 60 *American Journal of Public Health* 2229; W. Haddon, 'Reducing the Damage of Motor-Vehicle Use' (1975) 77 *Technology Review* 1.

59 P. Barry, 'Individual versus Community Orientation in the Prevention of Injury' (1975) 4 *Preventive Medicine* 47.

60 P. Waller, 'Injury as Disease' (1987) 19 *Accident Analysis and Prevention* 13 at 17.

61 Haddon and Baker, 'Injury Control,' 113.

62 L. Robertson, *Injuries* (Lexington: D.C. Heath, 1983) 83.

63 Leon Robertson, an epidemiologist, notes that much scientific research involves investigations into fault and human error and 'this obsession with blame is at least partly the result of a legal system that focuses on allocation of compensation and punishment according to the intent or fault of the persons immediately involved'; ibid., 1.

64 Epidemiologist Julian Waller, for example, has recently commented: 'Injury events may result simultaneously from individual flouting or ignoring of known risks for reasons of personal utility, individual misperception of risks that are totally unknown to the person and external application to the individual of risks because of social, governmental or corporate decision.' See Waller, 'Injury as Disease' (1987) 19 *Accident Analysis and Prevention* 13 at 15.

65 Taken in part from: W. Haddon, 'A Logical Framework' 199; W. Haddon, 'Options for the Prevention of Motor Vehicle Crash Injury' (1980) 16 *Israel Journal of Medical Science* 45.

66 W. Haddon and D. Klein, 'The Prospects for Safer Autos' (1965) 30 *Consumer Reports* 176.

67 W. Haddon, 'The Strategy of Preventive Medicine: Passive versus Active Approaches to Reducing Human Wastage' (1974) 14 *Journal of Trauma* 353 at 353.

68 Ibid.

69 'Modern societies long ago learned that, whenever practical, the best ways to reduce damage to people from hazards in the environment are those that do not require people to always be expert, alert and to take evasive action. Thus, we insulate household wires, rather than telling people never to touch them ... ; we purify water and pasteurize milk, rather than telling people they should always boil them to prevent illness'; W. Haddon, 'Options' 54–5.

70 US National Research Council, *Injury in America* (Washington: National Academy Press, 1985) 26ff, 40ff.

71 S. Peltzman, 'The Effects of Automobile Safety Regulation' (1975) 83 *Journal of Political Economy* 677. For a more thorough discussion of the Peltzman article and later articles see chapter 7, below.

72 *Ibid.*, 717.

73 See G.J.S. Wilde and G.A. Curry, 'Psychological Aspects of Road Research: A Study of the Literature, 1959–1968' (Ottawa: Transport Canada, 1970). There have been many articles by Wilde since then, the latest of which is 'Risk Homeostasis Theory and Traffic Accidents: Propositions, Deductions and Discussion of Dissension in Recent Reactions' (1988) 31 *Ergonomics* 441. Wilde is talking about unit of time, not unit of distance travelled. Even if this theory is correct, there are still benefits for travellers in having safer cars and highways. He is claiming risk homeostasis not for each individual driver, but for the aggregate of drivers.

74 D.H. Taylor, 'Drivers' Galvanic Skin Response and the Risk of Accidents' (1964) 7 *Ergonomics* 439 at 442.

75 J.G.U. Adams, *Risk and Freedom: The Record of Road Safety Regulation* (London: Transport Publishing Projects, 1985) 13; J.G.U. Adams, 'Smeed's Law, Seat Belts, and the Emperor's New Clothes,' in L. Evans, and R.C. Schwing, eds., *Human Behavior and Traffic Safety* (New York: Plenum Press, 1985) 193 at 217–26; J.G.U. Adams, 'Evaluating the Effectiveness of Road Safety Measures' (1988) 29 *Traffic Engineering and Control* 344; J.G.U. Adams, 'Risk Homeostasis and the Purpose of Safety Regulation' (1988) 31 *Ergonomics* 407 (Adams is cautious here: he states that 'the theory ... is plausible but untestable').

76 Adams, 'Smeed's Law' 217–26, and M. Mackay, 'Seat Belt Use under
    Voluntary and Mandatory Conditions and Its Effect on Casualties,' in
    L. Evans and R.C. Schwing, eds., *Human Behavior and Traffic Safety*
    (New York: Plenum Press, 1985) 260–2; see also L. Evans, 'Risk
    Homeostasis Theory and Traffic Accident Data' (1986) 6 *Risk Analysis*
    81; G.J.S. Wilde, 'Notes on the Interpretation of Traffic Accident Data
    and of Risk Homeostasis Theory: A Reply to L. Evans' (1986) 6 *Risk
    Analysis* 95; and L. Evans, 'Comments on Wilde's Notes on "Risk
    Homeostasis Theory and Traffic Accident Data"' (1986) 6 *Risk Analy-
    sis* 103.
77 K. Rumar, U. Berggrand, D. Jernberg, and U. Ytterbour, 'Driver
    Reaction to a Technical Safety Measure – Studded Tires' (1976) 18
    Human Factors 443.
78 L. Evans, 'Factors Controlling Traffic Crashes' (1987) 23 *Journal of
    Applied Behavioral Science* 201 at 209–11; see also F.M. Streff and E.S.
    Geller, 'An Experimental Test of Risk Compensation: Between-
    Subject Versus Within-Subject Analyses' (1988) 20 *Accident Analysis
    and Prevention* 277.
79 G. Blomquist, *The Regulation of Motor Vehicle and Traffic Safety* (Ameri-
    can Enterprise Institute, 1987) 103–5; G. Blomquist, 'A Utility Maxi-
    mization Model of Driver Traffic Safety Behavior' (1986) 18 *Accident
    Analysis and Prevention* 371; see also W.K. Viscusi, *Regulating Con-
    sumer Product Safety* (Washington, DC: American Institute for Public
    Policy Research, 1984).
80 J.L. Mashaw and D.L. Harfst, 'Regulation and Legal Culture: The
    Case of Motor Vehicle Safety' (1987) 4 *Yale Journal of Regulation*
    257.
81 P. Rock, *A View from the Shadows* (Oxford: Clarendon Press, 1986).
82 Canadian Sentencing Commission, *Sentencing Reform: A Canadian
    Approach* (Ottawa: Canadian Government Publishing Centre, 1986)
    134–45.
83 A.J. Reiss, 'Consequences of Compliance and Deterrence Models of
    Law Enforcement for the Exercise of Police Discretion' (1984) 47 *Law
    and Contemporary Problems* 83 at 122.
84 Ibid., 118.
85 These have been relatively constant over the years: 1,099,445 in 1975;
    1,268,653 in 1980; and 1,103,896 in 1985: based on statistics in *Ontario
    Motor Vehicle Accident Facts* (Ministry of Transportation and Com-
    munications), issues from 1974 to 1985. Ontario Highway Traffic Act

convictions for 1987 were 1,284,357: *1987 Ontario Road Safety Annual Report*, 60.

86 Department of Transport, *Road Traffic Law Review Report* (London: Her Majesty's Stationery Office, 1988) 25.

87 See K. Jobson and G. Ferguson, 'Toward a Revised Sentencing Structure for Canada' (1987) 66 *Canadian Bar Review* 1 at 43, note 133: 'It is estimated that 40% of court time is taken up with drinking-driving related offences; persons convicted of drinking and driving commonly comprise from 12–30% of admissions to provincial institutions.'

88 *Road Traffic Law Review Report* 112.

89 See, e.g., K.R. Williams and R. Hawkins, 'Perceptual Research on General Deterrence: A Critical Review' (1986) 20 *Law and Society Review* 545.

90 P.J. Cook, 'The Economics of Criminal Sanctions,' in Friedland, ed., *Sanctions and Rewards in the Legal System* 54. Similarly, Johannes Andenaes argues that 'just as fear enters the picture when people take a calculated risk in committing an offence, fear may also be an element in behavior which is not rationally motivated': Andenaes, 'The General Preventive Effects of Punishment' (1966) 114 *University of Pennsylvania Law Review* 949 at 955.

91 Report of the Canadian Sentencing Commission, *Sentencing Reform: A Canadian Approach* (Ottawa: Ministry of Supply and Services, 1986), 136–7. Compare a study done for the commission by Douglas Cousineau, quoted at 136: 'Drawing upon some nine bodies of research addressing the deterrence question, we contend that there is little or no evidence to sustain an empirically justified belief in the deterrent efficacy of legal sanctions.' Most experimental research bears on specific, not general deterrence: see J.P. Gibbs, 'Deterrence Theory and Research,' in G.B. Melton, ed., *Nebraska Symposium on Motivation, 1985: The Law as a Behavioral Instrument* (Lincoln: University of Nebraska Press, 1986) 113–14. For discussion of some of the difficulties in doing deterrence research, see R. Paternoster, 'Examining Three-Wave Deterrence Models: A Question of Temporal Order and Specification' (1988) 79 *Journal of Criminal Law and Criminology* 135.

92 A.F. Carr, J.F. Schnelle, and R.E. Kirchner, jr, 'Police Crackdowns and Slowdowns: A Naturalistic Evaluation of Changes in Police Traffic Enforcement' (1980) 2 *Behavioral Assessment* 33.

93 Ibid., 39.

94 Statistics from *Metropolitan Toronto Police Annual Report*, 22. However, the more serious traffic offences, that is, those under the Criminal Code, did not decrease anywhere near the decrease in Highway Traffic Act cases: they dropped from 28,952 to 27,393. It is hard to draw any firm conclusions because accident reporting requirements changed at the beginning of 1985 from $400 to $700 (see Ontario Regulation 489/84, s. 28, setting the $700 limit to take effect 1 January 1985). Thus it is not surprising that accident figures in Metro Toronto went down from 51,925 in 1984 to 42,721 in 1985. Figures from 1986, when enforcement was back to normal, show a decline in fatalities from 98 to 83, but personal injury accidents remained about the same (17,575 in 1986): *Metropolitan Toronto Police Annual Report*, 1986, 18.

95 Transport Canada Road Safety Report. *Effectiveness of Traffic Law Enforcement* (TP 1662), undated, probably 1973. See also R. Zylman, 'Drivers' Records: Are They a Valid Measure of Driving Behavior?' (1972) 4 *Accident Analysis and Prevention* 340: 'the traffic laws most often enforced may have little to do with collision involvement.'

96 Ibid., 36.

97 Ibid., 37.

98 Ibid., 34–5.

99 J.A. Gardiner, *Traffic and the Police: Variations in Law-Enforcement Policy* (Cambridge, Mass.: Harvard University Press, 1969) 162.

100 *R. v. Thomsen* [1988] 1 SCR 655; see also *R. v. Hufsky* [1988] 1 SCR 621 at 635, upholding random spot checks by Mr Justice Le Dain: 'What the material emphasizes is not only the seriousness of impaired driving, but the difficulty of detecting it by observation of the driving and the importance, in order to increase the effective deterrence of it, of increasing the perceived risk of its detection.'

101 P.J. Cook, 'The Economics of Criminal Sanctions' in Friedland, ed., *Sanctions and Rewards in the Legal System* 62ff. Compare A.M. Polinsky, *An Introduction to Law and Economics* (Boston: Little, Brown, 1983); R.A. Posner, 'An Economic Theory of the Criminal Law' (1985) 85 *Columbia Law Review* 1193; R.A. Posner, *Economic Analysis of Law*, 3rd ed. (Boston: Little, Brown, 1986).

102 Cook, 'The Economics of Criminal Sanctions' 63.

103 J.L. Miller and A.B. Anderson, 'Updating the Deterrence Doctrine' (1986) 77 *Journal of Criminal Law and Criminology* 418.

104 Ibid., 438.
105 See, generally, H.L. Ross, 'The Neutralization of Severe Penalties: Some Traffic Law Studies' (1976) 10 *Law and Society* 403 at 403: 'increases in formal penalties tend to be subverted by contrary adjustments in the behaviour of those who apply the law.'
106 As well as many writers: see, e.g., T. Honderich, *Punishment: The Supposed Justifications* (Harmondsworth: Penguin Books, 1984) 58 at 61–5 (flogging a parking offender would be morally unacceptable, even if it would clean up the city's parking problem). Some go much further: see, e.g., J.W. Morris, 'The Structure of Criminal Law and Deterrence' [1986] *Criminal Law Review* 524 at 526: 'A parking offender, for example, should not be subjected to punishment of such severity that it outweighs the harm that only one potential parking offender might do ... A system of deterrence works unfairly when it looks beyond a person's own past conduct to justify any punishment imposed on him.' See also A.H. Goldman, 'The Paradox of Punishment' (1979) 9 *Philosophy and Public Affairs* 42; J. Andenaes, 'The Morality of Deterrence' (1970) 37 *University of Chicago Law Review* 649.
107 Canadian Charter of Rights and Freedoms, Constitution Act, 1982, s. 12: 'Everyone has the right not to be subjected to any cruel and unusual treatment or punishment.'
108 *Smith v. The Queen* (1987), 34 CCC (3d) 97 at 139. See, generally, K. Roach, '*Smith* and the Supreme Court: Implications for Sentencing Policy and Reform' (1989) 11 *Supreme Court Law Review* 433.
109 R.A. Posner, 'An Economic Theory of the Criminal Law' (1985) 85 *Columbia Law Review* 1193 at 1206.
110 See S. Shavell, 'Criminal Law and the Optimal Use of Non-monetary Sanctions as a Deterrent' (1985) 85 *Columbia Law Review* 1232 at 1246.
111 See H.L. Ross, *Deterring the Drinking Driver: Legal Policy and Social Control*, revised ed. (Lexington, Mass.: D.C. Heath, 1984) 104–5, 110. See also H.L. Ross, 'Sociology and Legal Sanctions,' in Friedland, ed., *Sanctions and Rewards in the Legal System* 39–40.
112 Laboratory experiments with rodents and humans indicate that celerity is important for specific deterrence: see R.D. Clark, 'Celerity and Specific Deterrence: A Look at the Evidence' (1988) 30 *Canadian Journal of Criminology* 109.
113 J.Q. Wilson and R.J. Herrnstein, *Crime and Human Nature* (New York: Simon and Schuster, 1985) 397.

114 E. Vingilis et al. 'An Evaluation of the Deterrent Impact of Ontario's 12-Hour Licence Suspension Law' (1988) 20 *Accident Analysis and Prevention* 9.

115 Wilson and Herrnstein, *Crime and Human Nature* Appendix, 531.

116 See C.D. Stone, 'Choice of "Target" and other Law Enforcement Variables,' in Friedland, ed., *Sanctions and Rewards in the Legal System* 203.

117 Owners can, in certain cases, be charged under s. 181(1) of the Ontario Highway Traffic Act, as long as they consented to the driver's use of the car. But s. 181(2) removes from this provision most of the standard traffic violations (including, for example, speeding, seat-belt use and obeying traffic signs). The main effect of s. 181(1) appears to be to give the police a tactical advantage in enforcement: owners have to help with investigations or else face charges themselves. It seems that failure to remain is the principal offence for which police use s. 181. The Ontario Court of Appeal has found, however, that s. 181 infringes section 7 of the Charter and is therefore invalid: see *R. v. Pellerin, Lawyers Weekly* 3 February 1989. See also, to the same effect, *R. v. Burt* (1987), 38 CCC (3d) 299 (Sask. CA); cf. *R. v. Gray* (1988), 44 CCC (3d) 222 (Man. CA), upholding similar legislation under section 1 of the Charter. If the sections are stuck down they could be made constitutionally valid by eliminating the possibility of a prison sentence.

118 The Supreme Court of Canada has held that an absolute liability offence which carries a possible term of imprisonment violates s. 7 of the Charter: see *Reference re S. 94(2) of Motor Vehicle Act* [1985] 2 SCR 486.

119 P.F. Waller, 'The Highway Transportation System as a Commons: Implications for Risk Policy' (1986) 8 *Accident Analysis and Prevention* 417 at 423.

120 See A. Freiberg, 'Reconceptualizing Sanctions' (1987) 25 *Criminology* 223 at 235–6.

121 N. Walker, *Crime and Criminology: A Critical Introduction* (Oxford: Oxford University Press, 1987) 181. See G.M. Brown, 'Do Judicial "Scarlet Letters" Violate the Cruel and Unusual Punishments Clause of the Eighth Amendment?' (1988) 16 *Hastings Constitutional Law Quarterly* 115.

122 In Friedland, ed., *Sanctions and Rewards in the Legal System* 99.

123 D.T. Campbell and H.L. Ross, 'The Connecticut Crackdown on
    Speeding: Time Series Data in Quasi-Experimental Analysis' (1968–9)
    3 *Law and Society Review* 33, and G.V. Glass, 'Analysis of Data on the
    Connecticut Speeding Crackdown as a Time-Series Quasi-Experi-
    ment' (1968–9) 3 *Law and Society Review* 55.
124 Zimring, in Friedland, ed., *Sanctions and Rewards in the Legal System*
    100.
125 G. Kelling and A. Pate, *The Kansas City Preventative Patrol Experiment*
    (Washington, DC: Police Foundation, 1974), cited in ibid.
126 See L.W. Sherman and R.A. Berk, 'The Specific Deterrent Effects of
    Arrest for Domestic Assault' (1984) 49 *American Sociological Review*
    261, and R.A. Berk and P.J. Newton, 'Does Arrest Really Deter Wife
    Battery? An Effort to Replicate the Findings of the Minneapolis
    Spouse Abuse Experiment' (1985) 50 *American Sociological Review* 253.
    These studies are discussed in T.A.O. Endicott, 'The Criminality of
    Wife Assault' (1987) 45 *University of Toronto Faculty of Law Review* 355
    at 367.
127 Highway Traffic Amendment Act, SO 1975 (2nd sess.), c. 14. See now
    the Highway Traffic Act, RSO 1980, c. 198, s. 90.
128 Motor Vehicle Safety Regulations, SOR/70-487, s. 208(1). This regula-
    tion came into effect on 1 January 1971.
129 Nebraska and Massachusetts repealed their mandatory belt use laws
    in November 1986: *Insurance Institute for Highway Safety Status Report*
    21 no. 14 (13 December 1986) 10.
130 See R.J. Bonnie, 'The Efficacy of Law as a Paternalistic Instrument,' in
    G.B. Melton, ed., *Nebraska Symposium on Motivation, 1985: The Law as a
    Behavioral Instrument* (Lincoln: University of Nebraska Press, 1986)
    178. For 1987, 98.7 per cent of cars in Canada were fitted with shoul-
    der belts, and it is therefore now much easier to observe whether
    persons are complying with the law than when lap belts were widely
    used: Transport Canada Road Safety 'Leaflet' (TP 2436), January 1987.
131 *Status Report* 21 no. 14 (13 December 1986) 6. A survey in June 1988
    showed a Houston use rate of 66 per cent: *Status Report* 23 no. 9 (17
    September 1988) 6. For an analysis of differences in seat-belt use
    among fourteen Texas cities, including Houston, see N.H. Mounce
    and W.M. Hinshaw, 'Local Mandatory Usage Law (MUL) Enforce-
    ment Levels and Observed Safety Belt Use in Selected Texas Cities,'
    in *Proceedings*, 1988 Annual Conference of the AAAM in Seattle, 271.
    The authors conclude (281) that 'in general, it appears that enforce-

ment data, alone, are not sufficient to explain variations in safety belt use in different areas.'

132 The Alberta legislation was struck down as a violation of section 7 of the Canadian Charter of Rights and Freedoms by an Alberta Queen's Bench judge in February 1989 (*Regina v. Maier*): see *Globe and Mail*, 3 February 1989; (1989), 47 CCC(3d) 214. It is unlikely that the ruling will be upheld on appeal. What effect the ruling will have on enforcement, use rates, and injuries remains to be seen.

133 B.A. Jonah and J.J. Lawson, 'Safety Belt Use Rates and User Characteristics,' 1985 OECD Symposium, *The Effectiveness of Safety Belt Use Laws* (Washington, DC, 1985).

134 J.A. Pierce, 'Safety Benefits of the Seat Belt Legislation and Speed Limit Reduction in Ontario,' American Association for Automotive Medicine, *Proceedings*, 3–6 October 1979, Louisville, Kentucky, 242 at 243. Jonah and Lawson indicate that the use rate before the Ontario legislation was 24 per cent: see B.A. Jonah and J.J. Lawson, 'The Effectiveness of the Canadian Mandatory Seat Belt Use Laws' (1984) 16 *Accident Analysis and Prevention* 433 at 436.

135 Transport Canada, *Road Safety Annual Report 1986*, 11.

136 M. Mackay, 'Seat Belt Use under Voluntary and Mandatory Conditions and Its Effect on Casualties,' in L. Evans and R.C. Schwing, eds., *Human Behavior and Traffic Safety* (New York: Plenum Press, 1985) 260.

137 Ibid., 259.

138 *Status Report* 22 no. 3 (14 March 1987) 6.

139 See 1985 OECD Symposium, *The Effectiveness of Safety Belt Use Laws*.

140 *Status Report* 23 no. 9 (17 September 1988) 6.

141 *Status Report* 22 no. 3 (14 March 1987) 6. See also A.F. Williams, A.K. Lund, D.F. Preusser, and R.D. Blomberg, 'Results of a Seat Belt Use Law Enforcement Campaign in Elmira, New York' (1987) 19 *Accident Analysis and Prevention* 243. A rate of 89 per cent was achieved on a portion of New York's Thruway on 23 August 1988 as a result of police enforcement and publicity: *Status Report* 23 no. 9 (17 September 1988) 1.

142 *Status Report* 23 no. 6 (4 June 1988) 5.

143 See B.A. Jonah and B.A. Grant, 'Long-Term Effectiveness of Selective Traffic Enforcement Programs for Increasing Seat Belt Use' (1985) 70 *Journal of Applied Psychology* 257 at 257.

144 A. Lamb, *Seat Belt Awareness and Enforcement Pilot Project* (Vancouver:

Traffic Safety Education Department, Insurance Corporation of British Columbia), cited in Jonah and Grant, 'Effectiveness' 258.

145 Jonah and Grant, 'Effectiveness' 258. In another BC study Watson found that publicity of a thirty-fold increase in charges in a community resulted in an increase in compliance from 45 per cent to 71 per cent: R.E.L. Watson, 'The Effectiveness of Increased Police Enforcement as a General Deterrent' (1986) 20 *Law and Society Review* 293. See also M.C. Lai and H.S. Dalkie, 'An Evaluation of a Selective Traffic Enforcement Program to Increase Seat Belt Use Rates in Manitoba' in *Proceedings of the Fifth Canadian Multidisciplinary Road Safety Conference, Calgary, June, 1987*, 43.

146 Jonah and Grant, 'Effectiveness' 257–8.

147 Ibid., 260. The number of convictions in Ontario for failure to use a seat-belt increased from 35,000 in 1977 to 96,000 in 1978. Statistics are from Ministry of Transportation and Communications, *Annual Report 1978–79* 27.

148 Conversation with B. Jonah, Transport Canada, Ottawa, 8 March 1988. See C. Dussault, 'Meta-Analyse qualitative de Huit Programmes d'Application selective (P.A.S.) sur le Port de la Ceinture de Securité,' *Proceedings of the Fifth Multidisciplinary Road Safety Conference Calgary, June, 1987*, 32.

149 *Status Report* 23 no 4 (16 April 1988). All Canadian provinces permit primary enforcement.

150 B.J. Campbell, 'The Relationship of Seat Belt Law Enforcement to Level of Belt Use' (University of North Carolina Highway Safety Research Center, June 1987) 8.

151 *Status Report* 23 no. 1 (30 January 1988) 6. See, generally, A.C. Wagenaar et al., *Factors Related to Nonuse of Seat Belts in Michigan*, NHTSA: DOT HS 807 217, September 1987.

152 *Status Report* 21 no. 14 (13 December 1986) 5–6.

153 B.J. Campbell, 'Relationship' 8. Primary enforcement may have contributed to the relatively high use rates in North Carolina: see *Status Report* 24 no. 1 (28 January 1989) 4.

154 *Status Report* 22 no. 3 (14 March 1987) 5.

155 *Status Report* 21 no. 14 (13 December 1986) 6.

156 *Status Report* 22 no. 3 (14 March 1987) 5.

157 *Status Report* 21 no. 6 (17 May 1986) 1.

158 See C. Dussault, 'Meta-Analyse' 37.

159 See *1985 Federal Road Safety Annual Report*, 13. See also *1986 Annual Report*, 12; B.A. Grant, 'Effectiveness of an Industry Based Seat Belt Program: The Canadian Context,' in *Fourth Canadian Multidisciplinary Road Safety Conference, Montreal, May, 1985*, 191.

160 N.I. Bohlin, 'A Statistical Analysis of 28,000 Accident Cases with Emphasis on Occupant Restraint Value,' in *The Proceedings of the 11th Stapp Car Crash Conference*, Paper No. 670925, SAE, 1967.

161 G.M. Mackay, 'Seat Belts in Europe – Their Use and Performance in Collisions,' in *Human Collision: International Symposium on Occupant Restraint* (Toronto, 1981) 39 at 48.

162 OECD, Road Transport Research, *OECD Road Safety Research: A Synthesis* (Paris, 1986) 65. The evidence of insurance losses in the United States following adoption of mandatory seat-belt laws is ambiguous, according to a study by the Highway Loss Data Institute. A comparison of insurance losses before and after adoption of eight state mandatory seat-belt use laws shows no clear-cut reductions in the number of injury claims. The researchers stated that 'belts are much less effective in preventing relatively minor injuries than serious and fatal injuries and most insurance injury claims are for relatively minor, but often expensive, injuries'; see *Status Report* 23 no. 9 (17 September 1988) 6.

163 W.H. Rutherford et al., *The Medical Effects of Seat Belt Legislation in the United Kingdom* (London: HMSO, 1985) 85.

164 Ibid., 4.

165 J.A. Pierce presents evidence that both the speed limit reduction and the seat-belt law in Ontario improved traffic safety: 'Safety Benefits of the Seat Belt Legislation and Speed Limit Reduction in Ontario,' *Proceedings of the American Association of Automotive Medicine* Louisville, Kentucky, 1979.

166 Rutherford et al., *Medical Effects* 11.

167 Ibid., 85 and 139. A later study under way in the Rochester, New York, area is producing similar results. 'Preliminary analysis for the first six months of 1984 [the law was passed on 1 December 1984] and 1985 reveals that the number of hospital admissions declined by 18 per-cent. Average Injury Severity Score fell from 15.1 in 1984 to 13.0 in 1985, while belt use increased from 11 per cent to 72 per cent during the same period.' See J.D. States et al., 'The Effect of the New York State Safety Belt Law on Hospital Admissions in Monroe

County (Rochester) New York,' in *Proceedings of the American Association for Automotive Medicine, 30th Annual Conference, 1986*, 407. These results will then be compared to two other community studies being conducted in other areas of New York (410).

Injury severity score (ISS) is a composite indication of the total severity of one or more injuries received in an accident and can range from 1 to 75 (see Rutherford et al., *Medical Effects* 21). A similar study in fourteen Suffolk County hospitals in New York for the first half of 1985 found a 7 per cent decline in admissions to hospitals and a 23 per cent decrease in skull injuries compared to the same period in the previous year, and deaths in the county decreased by 18 per cent; *Status Report* 22 no. 8 (18 July 1987) 5.

An earlier Ontario study has reached similar conclusions about the effectiveness of seat-belt use. Dagnone and Siu compared medical services and disabilities for patients treated in southern Ontario for the year prior to and the year following implementation of the seat-belt laws. It was found that belted occupants' medical treatment averaged $228 per incident, while unbelted occupants' costs averaged $419. See L.E. Dagnone and T.O. Siu, 'Effect of Seat Belt Use on the Demand for Medical Services,' in *Proceedings of the International Symposium on Occupant Restraint 1981*, 14, discussed in J.D. States et al., 'The Effect' 408. See also A.K. Lund, J.P. Pollner, and A.F. Williams, 'Preliminary Estimates of the Effects of Mandatory Seat Belt Use Laws,' (1987) 19 *Accident Analysis and Prevention* 219.

A recent paper studied persons involved in motor vehicle injury events in the province of Quebec between March 1978 and December 1981 for which at least one occupant subsequently made an insurance claim to the provincial car insurance body. The report states that for the group of front-seat passenger victims involved in single-vehicle or two-car crashes, use of the seat-belt would have reduced by 77 per cent the proportion of those killed, reduced by 48 per cent the proportion of occupants severely injured, and increased the proportion who were not injured by 11 per cent. See C. Laverge-Nadeau et al., 'The Seat Belt: Its Effectiveness in Similar Motor Vehicle Occupant-Injury Events,' in *Proceedings of the Fifth Canadian Multidisciplinary Road Safety Conference, Calgary, June, 1987*, 1. See also H.S. Dalkie and W.N. Milligan, *The Impact of Bill 60: A Study to Evaluate the Effectiveness of Mandatory Seat Belt and Motorcycle Helmet Use Legislation in Manitoba* (University of Manitoba Road Safety Research Unit).

168 See articles by J.G.U. Adams and M. Mackay in L. Evans and R.C. Schwing, eds., *Human Behaviour and Traffic Safety* at 193 and 259.

169 J.G.U. Adams, 'The Efficacy of Seat Belt Legislation: A Comparative Study of Road Accident Fatality Statistics from 18 Countries,' Occasional Paper No. 38, (London: University College, 1981), cited by M. Mackay in ibid., 261.

170 L. Evans, P. Wasielewski, and C.R. Ban Buseck, 'Compulsory Seat Belt Usage and Driver Risk-Taking Behavior' (1982) 24 *Human Factors* 41, cited by M. Mackay in ibid., 262. Cf. G. Blomquist, 'A Utility Maximization Model of Driver Traffic Safety Behavior' (1986) 18 *Accident Analysis and Prevention* 371, who argues (at 373) that there will be some risk compensation with respect to the use of seat-belts: 'Risk Compensation (or offsetting behavior or compensating feedback) is a normal response to changes in the safety environment in the context of a simple economic model of individual utility maximization.' Blomquist examines three safety belt studies and states (374): 'Each of the three safety belt use studies finds use determined by factors that correspond to factors in the driver utility maximization model. Belt use is found to be greater the larger are the net private benefits of use.' See also P.S. McCarthy, 'Seat Belt Usage Rates: A Test of Peltzman's Hypothesis' (1986) 18 *Accident Analysis and Prevention* 425, where it is argued that individuals travelling more risky environments are more likely to use their seat-belts.

171 M. Mackay in Evans and Schwing, eds., *Human Behavior and Traffic Safety* 262. Similarly, the report of the 1985 British government study discussed above held that the risk homeostasis theory 'has, at least in the Canadian context, been found to be unsupported by direct observations of driver behaviour'; Rutherford et al., *Medical Effects* 8. See also B.A. Jonah and J.J. Lawson, 'The Effectiveness of the Canadian Mandatory Seat Belt Use Laws' (1984) 16 *Accident Analysis and Prevention* 433 at 448.

172 A. Fleming, ed., *Highway Loss Data Institute: A Profile of the Organization* (Washington, DC: Highway Loss Data Institute, 1987) 16.

173 B. O'Neill, A.K. Lund, P. Zador, and S. Ashton, 'Mandatory Belt Use and Driver Risk-Taking: An Empirical Evaluation of the Risk-Compensation Hypothesis,' in Evans and Schwing, eds., *Human Behavior and Traffic Safety* 93. The driver behaviour examined included travel speeds, following headway, turning headway, and response to yellow signals.

174 OECD, *Synthesis* 65.

175 Jonah and Lawson, 'The Effectiveness of the Canadian Mandatory Seat Belt Use Laws' 448.

176 See F. McKenna in Evans and Schwing, eds., *Human Behavior and Traffic Safety* 147.

177 See A.K. Lund and B. O'Neill, 'Perceived Risks and Driving Behavior' (1986) 18 *Accident Analysis and Prevention* 367 at 369.

178 See *Status Report* 24 no. 1 (28 January 1989) 7.

179 *Status Report* 22 no. 14 (26 December, 1987) 10, and 23 no. 1 (30 January 1988) 6. See, generally, J.P. Rothe, *Never Say Always: Perspectives on Safety Belt Use* (New Brunswick, NJ: Transaction Publishers, 1988).

180 *Status Report* 23 no. 3 (14 March 1988) 7.

181 *Status Report* 23 no. 1 (30 January 1988) 6. See also Campbell and Campbell in *Status Report* 22 no. 13 (5 December 1987).

182 OECD, *Synthesis* 66.

183 This may not be true for increasing the compliance rate for teenagers, who now tend to belt up less frequently than the general population; see D.F. Preusser, A.F. Williams, and A.K. Lund, 'The Effect of New York's Seat Belt Use Law on Teenage Drivers' (1987) 19 *Accident Analysis and Prevention* 73. See, generally, D.F. Preusser, et al., 'Belt Use by High-Risk Drivers before and after New York's Seat Belt Use Law' (1988) 20 *Accident Analysis and Prevention* 245 at 249: 'those drivers most at risk of crashing are least likely to comply with the law.'

184 *Status Report* 21 no. 14 (13 December 1986) 6, and 22 no. 3 (14 March 1987) 6.

185 *Status Report* 23 no. 4 (16 April 1988) 4.

186 *Status Report* 22 no. 12 (21 November 1987) 1-3; see also *Status Report* 22 no. 7 (27 June 1987) 1.

187 *Status Report* 23 no. 9 (17 September 1988) 6.

188 *Status Report* 23 no. 4 (16 April 1988) 2.

189 *Status Report* 23 no. 10 (15 October 1988) 4.

190 *Status Report* 23 no. 2 (20 February 1988).

191 See *Status Report* 23 no. 8 (13 August 1988) 3. The extension seems to have had the desired effect. A sevenfold increase in the production of airbag-equipped cars will occur in the 1990 model year: see *Status Report* 23 no. 11 (3 December 1988) 1.

192 See K.C. Miller, 'Deflating the Airbag Pre-Emption Controversy' (1988) 37 *Emory Law Journal* 897 at 907.

193 Ibid., 908.

194 See *Status Report* 24 no. 4 (22 April 1989) 3: 'Now it's official. The federal regulation requiring automatic restraints for front seat occupants is permanent. Starting in September of this year all new cars must be equipped with automatic seat belts or air bags.'

195 *Ontario Motor Vehicle Accident Facts*, 1986, 60.

196 Transportation Research Board, *55: A Decade of Experience*, Special Report 204 (Washington, DC, 1984), 140–1. Oklahoma and South Dakota passed laws protecting speeding violations from public scrutiny, so that drivers could not be penalized by their insurance companies.

197 Ibid., 163.

198 *Globe and Mail*, 21 March 1987, A7.

199 President Reagan said that he had vetoed the bill because of the $88 billion in highway and mass transit improvement funding that was included: *Globe and Mail*, 3 April 1987, A10.

200 *Status Report* 23 no. 4 (16 April 1988) 3. Including up to twenty states that could be part of a four-year 65-mph demonstration program for roads that meet Interstate standards: see *Status Report* 22 no. 14 (26 December 1987) 6. The withholding of federal highway funds does not apply to the 65-mph limit: *Status Report* 23 no. 7 (9 July 1988) 3.

201 Provincial Ministry of Transportation survey, reported in *Toronto Star*, 6 January 1987, A9.

202 *55: A Decade of Experience*, 137.

203 P. Philibert, *Rapport du Comité sur les Limites de Vitesse* (Quebec: Ministère des Transports, 1987) 2.

204 D. Shinar and A.J. McKnight, 'The Effects of Enforcement and Public Information on Compliance,' in Evans and Schwing, eds., *Human Behavior and Traffic Safety* 385 at 392.

205 E. Hauer, F.J. Ahlin, and J.S. Bowser, *The Effect of Speed Enforcement on Driver Speed Choice* (Transport Canada, 1980) 2.

206 Ibid., 2–3.

207 *55: A Decade of Experience*, 147. See also D.T. Campbell and H.L. Ross, 'The Connecticut Crackdown on Speeding: Time-Series Data in Quasi-Experimental Analysis' (1968) 3 *Law and Society Review* 33.

208 *55: A Decade of Experience* 13 and 147. The estimate was based on
     highways that were subject to the 55-mph limit.
209 Ibid., 158.
210 Ibid., 159.
211 *Status Report* 22, no. 14 (26 December 1987) 1. See also *Status Report*
     23, no. 3 (14 March 1988) 7, which also does not control for exposure.
212 More recent Department of Transport evidence, again not controlling
     for exposure, shows that traffic deaths increased by 18 per cent in the
     first nine months of 1987 for the thirty-seven states with a 65-mph
     limit. But the evidence also shows a 17 per cent increase in the states
     that still have a 55-mph limit. See *Status Report* 23 no. 7 (9 July 1988)
     3. See also *Status Report* 23 no. 8 (13 August 1988) 1 and 24 no. 1 (28
     January 1989) 1, showing that while there was a rise in deaths on
     interstates with a 65-mph limit, deaths fell in the same states on other
     roads in those states.
213 J.H. Hedlund, 'Recent U.S. Traffic Fatality Trends,' in Evans and
     Schwing, eds., *Human Behavior and Traffic Safety* 7 at 8–9.
214 There was a reduction in fatalities from 3.25 per 100 million km in
     1973 to 2.75 in 1974: *Ontario Motor Vehicle Accident Facts, 1974.*
215 J.G.U. Adams, *Risk and Freedom* (Cardiff: Transport Publishing
     Projects, 1985) 100.
216 See J.A. Pierce, 'Safety Benefits of the Seat Belt Legislation and Speed
     Limit Reduction in Ontario' (1979) *Proceedings of the American Associa-
     tion of Automotive Medicine* (Louisville) 242.
217 See Jim Kenzie, 'Do Highway Speed Limits Save Lives?' *Toronto Star,*
     4 October 1986, J1.
218 *55: A Decade of Experience* 69.
219 R.W. Crandall, H.K. Gruenspecht, T.E. Keeler, and L.B. Lave, *Regulat-
     ing the Automobile* (Washington, DC: Brookings Institution, 1986) 155.
220 Ibid., 65.
221 Ibid., 67.
222 See *55: A Decade of Experience* 38–40, for a discussion of the link
     between speed and safety and of the interaction between speed and
     other factors. See also US Department of Transportation, *Synthesis of
     Safety Research Related to Traffic Control and Roadway Elements,* Vol. II
     (Washington, DC, 1982) 17-2. And see OECD, *Synthesis* 71–72: 'A
     number of studies indicate that, other things being equal a reduction
     in the mean speed of traffic gives rise to a reduced accident rate and
     lower accident severity. A rough quantification of these effects, based

on the results of Swedish research, but consistent with and often more conservative than similar estimates from other countries, may be stated as follows: the percentage drop in accident rates outside of built-up areas is n times the percentage drop in mean speed where $n = 4$ for fatal accidents, $n = 3$ for personal injury accidents, and $n = 2$ for all accidents.'

223 US *Synthesis*, 17–2.

224 Ibid., 17–6.

225 Ibid., 17–6. See also E. Hauer, 'Accidents, Overtaking and Speed Control' (1971) 3 *Accident Analysis and Prevention* 1.

226 OECD, *Synthesis* 72.

227 *55: A Decade of Experience*, 241–2.

228 Ibid., 136. See also US *Synthesis* 17–7.

229 US *Synthesis* 17–7.

230 Philibert, *Rapport du Comité sur les Limites de Vitesse* 26–7.

231 *Status Report* 22 no. 14 (18 July 1987) 3.

232 *Status Report* 22 no. 8 (26 December 1987) 5. See also *Status Report* 23 no. 3 (14 March 1988): those travelling more than 70 mph in South Carolina doubled from 12 per cent to 24 per cent between June 1987 and January 1988.

233 *Status Report* 22 no. 12 (21 November 1987) 6. Some trucks are even using radar jammers: *Status Report* 22 no. 11 (17 October 1987) 4. In one study, 54 per cent of tractor trailers travelling over 70 mph abruptly slowed when police radar was activated: *Status Report* 23 no. 7 (9 July 1988) 7–8. The governor of Michigan said that he would not agree to raising the limit to 65 unless this was coupled with a ban on radar detectors: *Status Report* 22 no. 10 (19 September 1987) 4. The new Multinova police radar system used in some Canadian jurisdictions (e.g. Alberta and British Columbia) avoids driver detection but relies on charging the registered owner (see *Globe and Mail*, 10 November 1987), which may violate the Charter of Rights: see *R. v. Burt* (1987), 38 CCC (3d) 299 (Sask. CA); see also *R. v. Pellerin*, 3 February 1989, *Lawyers Weekly*, (Ontario CA).

234 *Status Report* 23 no. 11 (3 December 1988) 3.

235 Ibid., 2.

236 The first study is M.L. Chipman and P.P. Morgan, 'The Predictive Value of Driver Demerit Points in Ontario,' *Proceedings of the American Association for Automotive Medicine*, Toronto, 12–14 September 1974, 399. The later study is M.L. Chipman, 'The Role of Exposure,

Experience and Demerit Point Levels in the Risk of Collision,' 14
Accident Analysis and Prevention 475. Roger Cramton points out that
studies showing a relationship between accidents and traffic violations may be suspect: an artificial correlation may arise because many
accidents result in at least one driver being prosecuted; R.C. Cramton, 'Driver Behavior and Legal Sanctions: A Study of Deterrence'
(1969) 67 *Michigan Law Review* 421 at 436–7.

237 US *Synthesis* 17.
238 *55: A Decade of Experience* 230. See also 6–8, for a discussion of federal
efforts to force states to enforce the limit, and 149, on the role of local
as opposed to state enforcement.
239 See Paul Weston, *The Police Traffic Control Function* (a leading police
manual) 4th ed. (1978) 119: 'The ideal situation is to have realistic
speed laws and a policy of little or no tolerance.'
240 OECD, *Synthesis* 72.
241 'Caution: Higher Speed on Rural Interstates Won't End There,' *Status
Report* 22 no. 1 (24 January 1987) 5. See also *55: A Decade of Experience*
11–12.
242 See Weston, *The Police Traffic Control Function* 27.
243 See *Globe and Mail*, 26 March 1988.
244 *Toronto Star*, 11 May 1988. Radar cannot be used in California unless
the posted speed limits have been justified by an engineering and
traffic survey: see S. Spitz, 'Speed vs. Speed Limits in California
Cities' (1984) *ITE Journal* (Japan) 42.
245 Despite some apparent recent reductions, drunk driving remains the
most important identifiable factor in fatal traffic accidents. In the
United States in 1980, 50.1 per cent of fatally injured drivers tested for
alcohol had BACs of over 100 mg/100 ml, and in 1983 46.4 per cent
had such BACs: J. Fell, 'Alcohol Involvement in United States Traffic
Accidents: Where It Is Changing,' in S. Kaye, ed., *Alcohol, Drugs and
Traffic Safety: Proceedings of the 9th International Conference on Alcohol,
Drugs and Traffic Safety* (Washington, DC: NHTSA, 1985) 453.
   In 1980 in Canada, 47.9 per cent of fatally injured automobile drivers
tested for alcohol had BACs over 80 mg/100 ml; in 1983, 42.6 per cent;
in 1985, 41.3 per cent: D. Beirness et al., *Alcohol and Fatal Road
Accidents in Canada: A Statistical Look at Its Magnitude and Persistence*
(Ottawa: Department of Justice, 1985) 24; G. Haas et al., 'Alcohol Use
by Persons Fatally Injured in Motor Vehicle Accidents: 1984,' *Final
Report* (Ottawa: Transport Canada, 1985) Table A-2; A. Donelson et

al., *Alcohol Use by Persons Fatally Injured in Motor Vehicle Accidents*
(Ottawa: Traffic Injury Research Foundation of Canada, 1986) Table
A-2.

The presence of alcohol in these fatal accidents does not necessarily
mean that drunk driving 'caused' the crash. Traffic accidents are the
result of many interactive conditions, and the most effective means of
prevention is not always one that addresses the primary causal
determinant of the accident.

246 Mercer, 'The Counterattack Program,' in *Counterattack Traffic Research
Papers* (Vancouver: Ministry of the Attorney-General, 1984) 2; *Correc-
tional Services in Canada 1980–81* (Ottawa: Solicitor-General of Canada) 32, quoted in K. Jobson and G. Ferguson, 'Towards a Revised
Sentencing Structure for Canada' (1987) 66 *Canadian Bar Review* 1 at
43; R. Voas, 'Evaluation of Jail as a Penalty for Drunk Driving' (1986)
2 *Alcohol, Drugs and Driving Abstracts and Reviews* 47 at 63. One
Canadian study estimates that the average cost of a drunk driving
conviction for the criminal justice system is over $700: W. Mercer,
'The Relationships among DWI Charges, Police Visibility and Alcohol-
Related Casualty Traffic Accidents,' in *Counterattack Traffic Research
Papers* 119.

247 H.L. Ross, 'Traffic Law Violation: A Folk Crime' (1960) 8 *Social
Problems* 231. A recent British policy document has noted that the
conduct that gives rise to traffic offences 'may involve no more than
carelessness, misjudgment, a lapse of concentration, a failure to be
aware of or understand a relatively technical requirement – failings
which are not in themselves regarded as morally reprehensible':
Department of Transport, *Road Traffic Law Review Report* (London:
HMSO, 1988) 19. Sociologist Joseph Gusfield has studied the symbolic
and normative implications of the use of criminal sanctions and the
cultural image of the killer drunk: see generally, J. Gusfield, 'Social
and Cultural Contexts of the Drinking-Driving Event,' *Journal of
Studies on Alcohol* Supp. 10 (July 1985) 75; *The Culture of Public Problems: Drinking Driving and the Symbolic Order* (Chicago: Chicago
University Press, 1981).

On the possible role of a large variety of attitudinal and cultural
factors in recent reductions in drunk driving, see J.R. Snortum,
'Controlling the Alcohol-Impaired Driver in Scandinavia and the
United States: Simple Deterrence and Beyond' (1984) 12 *Journal of
Criminal Justice* 131; D. Berger and J. Snortum, 'A Structural Model of

Drinking and Driving: Alcohol Consumption, Social Norms and
Moral Commitments' (1986) 24 *Criminology* 139; J.R. Snortum, 'De-
terrence of Alcohol-Impaired Driving: An Effect in Search of a
Cause,' in M.D. Laurence, J.R. Snortum, and F.E. Zimring, eds., *Social
Control of the Drinking Driver* (Chicago: University of Chicago Press,
1988) 189; J. Gusfield, 'The Control of Drinking-Driving in the United
States: A Period of Transition?' in ibid., 109.

248 The landmark study in determining the correlation between high
blood alcohol levels and risk of traffic accidents is R. Borkenstein et
al., *The Role of the Drinking Driver in Traffic Accidents* (Bloomington:
Department of Police Administration, Indiana University, 1964).

249 Donelson and Beirness argue that objective per se laws blur a distinc-
tion between science and law. They state: 'Scientific research findings
are probabilistic, indicating the *likelihood* of their being correct. Thus,
there always exists the possibility of exceptions to the rule. The rules
of Law, especially as applied to adjudicating the guilt or innocence of
individuals charged with committing an offence, operate on an
individual, or *case-specific* basis': A. Donelson and D. Beirness, *Legislative Issues Related to Drinking and Driving* (Ottawa: Department of
Justice, 1985) 54–5. See also L. Lanza-Kaduce and D. Bishop, 'Legal
Fictions and Criminology: The Jurisprudence of Drunk Driving'
(1986) 77 *Journal of Criminal Law and Criminology* 358. Experiments
suggest, however, that 90 per cent or more of people can predict
when they reach prohibited BACs: N. Russ et al., 'Estimating Alcohol
Impairment in the Field: Implications for Drunken Driving' (1986) 47
Journal of Studies on Alcohol 237 at 239.

250 In *R. v. Phillips* (1988), 42 CCC (3d) 150, the Ontario Court of Appeal
upheld a presumption in the Criminal Code that the results of a
breathalyser analysis, in the absence of evidence to the contrary, were
proof of the accused's blood alcohol level at the time the driving
offence was committed. See also J.B. Jacobs 'The Law and Criminology of Drunk Driving' (1988) 10 *Crime and Justice* 171 at 186–92.

251 For example, data from 12,000 apprehended Canadian drivers
indicated an average BAC of 172 mg/100 ml, and 70 per cent of the
cases had BACs greater than 150 mg/100 ml, even though the legal
limit is 80 mg/100 ml: D.G. Alford, *Impaired Driving: Canadian Statistics and International Legislative Comparisons* (Ottawa: Research Branch,
Department of Justice, 1985) 11. Such a conscious or unconscious

tolerance policy may actually target those drivers most likely to be involved in serious traffic accidents. For example, in 1984, of fatally injured automobile drivers tested for alcohol, 31.6 per cent had BACs over 150 mg/100 ml, 11.1 per cent had BACs between 81 and 150 mg/100 ml, and 3.8 per cent had BACs between 50 and 80 mg/100 ml: G. Haas et al., *Alcohol Use by Persons Fatally Injured in Motor Vehicle Accidents: 1984* (Ottawa: Transport Canada, 1985) A-2.

252 H.L. Ross, 'Law, Science and Accidents: The British Road Safety Act of 1967' (1973) 2 *Journal of Legal Studies* 1 at 20ff; B. Carr et al., 'The Canadian Breathalizer Legislation: An Inferential Evaluation,' in S. Israelstam and S. Lambert, eds., *Alcohol, Drugs and Traffic Safety: Proceedings of the Sixth International Conference on Alcohol, Drugs and Traffic Safety* (Toronto: Addiction Research Foundation, 1975) 679 at 683; L.W. Chambers et al., 'The Epidemiology of Traffic Accidents and the Effect of the 1969 Breathalyser Law in Canada,' in ibid., 689 at 693. Similar results were observed after Maine's passage of a per se sanction. R. Hingson et al. 'Effects of Maine's 1981 and Massachusetts' 1982 Driving-under-the-Influence Legislation (1987) 77 *American Journal of Public Health* 593.

253 This is the general conclusion reached by Ross in his comprehensive international survey of similar interventions. See H.L. Ross, *Deterring the Driving Driver*, revised ed., (Lexington: D.C. Heath, 1984): 'My conclusion is that the main limitation of attempts to deter drunk driving lies in the failure of all jurisdictions to date to raise the actual risk of punishment to a level that cannot be overlooked by potential violators' (xxvii).

254 In Canada, for example, the severity of punishment for drinking and driving was, if anything, reduced, as the offence of intoxicated driving, with its mandatory minimum penalty of imprisonment for thirty days, was abolished and the new offence of driving with a BAC over 80 mg/100 ml carried a minimum penalty of only a $50 fine: RSC 1968–9, c. 38, s. 16. See also Road Traffic Act 1960, 8 & 9 Eliz. 2, ch. 16, s. 6; Road Safety Act 1967, ch. 30, s. 1.

255 Ross, *Deterring the Drinking Driver* 118–20; L. Robertson et al., 'Jail Sentences for Driving while Intoxicated in Chicago: A Judicial Policy that Failed' (1973) 8 *Law and Society Review* 55; H.L. Ross and J.P. Foley, 'Judicial Disobedience of the Mandate to Imprison Drunk Drivers' (1987) 21 *Law and Society Review* 315. On the distortion effects

of increased severity for traffic offences in general, see H.L. Ross,
'The Neutralization of Severe Penalties: Some Traffic Law Studies'
(1970) 10 *Law and Society Review* 403.

256 R. Homel, 'Penalties and the Drunk-Driver: A Study of One Thousand Offenders' (1981) 14 *Australian and New Zealand Journal of
Criminology* 225.

257 C. Falcowski, 'The Impact of Two Day Jail Sentences for Drunk
Drivers in Hennepin County, Minnesota' (1986) 17 *Journal of Safety
Research* 33. After the introduction of policy to jail first-time drunk
driving offenders, a 20 per cent reduction in injury accidents was
observed, although enforcement activities and arrests also increased
during this time, suggesting that both severity and certainty of
punishment were increased. Single-vehicle night time accidents and
overall fatal crashes did not decline in the three years after Massachusetts introduced an offence of vehicular homicide under the
influence, with the severe sanctions of a mandatory ten-year licence
suspension and a minimum of one year's imprisonment: see R.
Hingson et al., 'Effects of Legislation' 593.

258 B. Carr et al. 'The Canadian Breathalizer Legislation: An Inferential
Evaluation,' in S. Israelstam and S. Lambert, eds., *Alcohol, Drugs and
Traffic Safety: Proceedings of the Sixth International Conference on Alcohol,
Drugs and Traffic Safety* (Toronto: Addiction Research Foundation,
1975) 684, 687; H.L. Ross, 'Law, Science and Accidents' (1973) 2
Journal of Legal Studies 1.

259 During the Phoenix ASAP, arrests for drunk driving were increased
between 60 and 75 per cent, yet only 29 per cent of a sample interviewed believed that their chances of being stopped by the police
after drinking and driving were high. These perceptions were, in fact,
realistic, as, even during peak enforcement, drunk driving arrests
represented only 2.9 per cent of the estimated number of all the
licensed drivers in the city. See T. Clay and P. Swenson, 'Selective
Enforcement of Drunken Driving in Phoenix, Arizona' (1978) 10
Journal of Safety Research 130 at 134, 136; W. Mercer, 'The Relationships among Driving while Impaired Charges, Police Visibility and
Alcohol-Related Casualty Traffic Accidents,' in *Counterattack Traffic
Research Papers* (Vancouver: Ministry of the Attorney-General, 1984)
119; W. Mercer, 'The Relationship among Driving while Impaired
Charges, Police Drinking-Driving Roadcheck Activity, Media Cover-

age and Alcohol-Related Casualty Traffic Accidents' (1985) 17 *Accident Analysis and Prevention* 467.

260 Liban et al., 'The Canadian Drinking Driving Countermeasure Experience' (1987) 19 *Accident Analysis and Prevention* 159 at 164; R. Borkenstein, 'A Panoramic View of Alcohol, Drugs and Traffic Safety' (1982) 16 *Police* 6 at 11; H.L. Ross, 'Sociology and Legal Sanctions,' in M.L. Friedland, ed., *Sanctions and Rewards in the Legal System: A Multidisciplinary Approach* (Toronto: University of Toronto Press, 1989) 46–47. A Canadian study based on night-time roadside surveys estimated the risk of apprehension to be 1 in 514 impaired trips or 1 in every 2,575 impaired kilometres: J. Lawson, 'Calculation of Chance of Arrest for Alcohol Impairment,' Transport Canada Memorandum, 25 January 1983, as quoted in E. Vingilis and V. Vingilis, 'The Importance of Roadside Screening for Impaired Drivers in Canada' (1987) 29 *Canadian Journal of Criminology* 17 at 22. One American study assessed the probability of arrest to be 1 in 200 impaired trips but was based on the unrealistic assumption that all available police officers will watch for drunk drivers: G. Beitel et al., 'Probability of Arrest while Driving under the Influence of Alcohol' (1975) 36 *Journal of Studies on Alcohol* 109.

261 H.L. Ross, 'Deterrence Regained: The Cheshire Constabulary's Breathalyser Blitz' (1977) 6 *Journal of Legal Studies* 241 at 245. The level of breath testing during the blitz was six times the national average: Ross, *Deterring the Drinking Driver* 73. See also H.L. Ross 'Britain's Christmas Crusade against Drinking and Driving' (1987) 48 *Journal of Studies on Alcohol* 476, for a somewhat similar and more recent experience involving publicity, threats of increased severity, and somewhat more moderate increases in breath testing.

262 R. Voas and J. Hause, 'Deterring the Drinking Driver: The Stockton Experience' (1987) 19 *Accident Analysis and Prevention* 81 at 84–6, 89.

263 T. Epperlein, 'Initial Deterrent Effects of the Crackdown on Drinking Drivers in the State of Arizona' (1987) 19 *Accident Analysis and Prevention* 285 at 301. This study does not address the effects of increased enforcement of the law but supports the general consensus 'that immediate deterrence result[s] from the publicized and notorious threat of apprehension surrounding the law's inception and not from the legal threat it presented.'

264 See ibid., 285 at 300ff. An objective liability and blood testing law that

was introduced in New Zealand with little publicity had no apparent
impact on drunk driving indicators: see P. Hurst, 'Blood Test Legislation in New Zealand' (1978) 10 *Accident Analysis and Prevention* 287.
On the positive role of publicity from civil libertarian criticisms of the
enforcement of drunk driving laws, see Ross, *Deterring the Drinking
Driver* chapters 4 and 5.

265 Liban et al., 'Countermeasure Experience' 159 at 165ff.
266 Jonah and Wilson report that in its first year of operation, 132,555
cars were stopped, spot-checks were carried out sixteen hours per
day, and only 1.2 per cent of drivers were breath-tested at the roadside: 'Improving the Effectiveness of Drinking-Driving Enforcement
through Increased Efficiency' (1983) 25 *Accident Analysis and Prevention* 463 at 466. See also E. Vingilis et al., 'Comparison of Age and Sex
Characteristics of Police-Suspected Impaired Drivers and Roadside-
Surveyed Impaired Drivers' (1982) 14 *Accident Analysis and Prevention*
425 at 426, who reported that during a year of the operation of the
RIDE program in Etobicoke only 1.1 per cent of drivers stopped were
breath-tested at the roadside.
267 Based on telephone interviews before and after implementation of
the RIDE program, respondents did not believe that their own risk of
apprehension for drunk driving had increased, although they were
willing to admit that the risk of apprehension may have increased for
others: C. Liban et al., *Drinking-Driving Countermeasure Review: The
Canadian Experience* (Toronto: Addiction Research Foundation, 1985)
102, 107.
268 I. Kearns et al., 'An Overview of the Random Breath Testing Trial in
New South Wales,' in P. Noordzij and R. Roszbach, eds., *Alcohol,
Drugs and Traffic Safety: Proceedings of the Tenth International Conference
on Alcohol, Drugs and Traffic Safety* (Amsterdam: Excerpta Medica,
1987) 429–30. For a very helpful survey of random breath testing in
Australia and other issues relating to traffic accidents, see R. Homel
and P. Wilson, *Death and Injuries on the Road: Critical Issues for Legislative Action and Law Enforcement* (Australian Capital Territory: Australian Institute of Criminology, 1987).
269 The percentage of late-night single-vehicle accidents on the back
streets increased from 30 to 46 per cent of such accidents: J. McLean
and O. Holubowycz, 'Side-Effects of Random Breath Testing by the
Police,' in Noordzij and Roszbach eds., *Alcohol, Drugs and Traffic
Safety* 441.

270 Experimental studies estimate that police fail to detect drinking in drivers at or just over the legal BAC limit by the use of visual clues between 50 and 95 per cent of the time: see R. Voas, 'Emerging Technologies for Controlling the Drunk Driver,' in M. Laurence, J. Snortum, and F. Zimring, eds., *Social Control of the Drinking Driver* (Chicago: University of Chicago, 1988) 347–8. Passive alcohol sensors can improve detection without requiring intrusion of random breath testing: I. Jones and A. Lund, 'Detection of Alcohol-Impaired Drivers Using a Passing Alcohol Sensor' (1986) 14 *Journal of Police Science and Administration* 153.

271 A 33 per cent reduction in night-time fatalities was observed following the introduction of random breath testing in the state of Victoria. Subsequent campaigns yielded between 18 and 24 per cent reduction in night-time serious-casualty accidents: see M. Armour et al., 'Random breath Testing in Victoria' in Laurence et al., eds., *Social Control* 434–7; see also in the same book H.L. Ross, 'Deterrence-Based Policies in Britain, Canada and Australia' 72ff.

272 J. Jacobs and N. Strasser, 'Mass Investigations without Individualized Suspicion: A Constitutional and Policy Critique of Drunk Driving Roadblocks' (1985) 18 *University of California Davis Law Review* 595.

273 *R. v. Hufsky* [1988] 1 SCR 621; *R. v. Thomsen* [1988] 1 SCR 640; *R. v. Seo* (1986), 25 CCC (3d) 385 (Ont. CA). The California Supreme Court, in *Ingersoll v. Palmer* (1987), 43 Cal. (3d) 1321, upheld sobriety checkpoints when they do not interfere with individuals' lives any more than necessary: see, generally, M.R. Soble, 'Clearing the Roadblocks to Sobriety Checkpoints' (1988) 21 *Journal of Law Reform* 489.

274 An evaluation of the non-punitive twelve-hour licence suspension in Ontario suggests that at best it may have had a small short-term effect in reducing alcohol-related fatalities: E. Vingilis, 'An Evaluation of the Deterrent Impact of Ontario's Twelve Hour License Suspension Law' (1988) 20 *Accident Analysis and Prevention* 9.

275 G. Tufts and W. Beckett, 'The Administrative Sanction Countermeasure to Impaired Driving,' *Fourth Canadian Multidisciplinary Road Safety Conference* (Montreal, 1985) 244.

276 In Sweden during the first two years of random breath testing, over one million drivers were tested, with only two in every thousand drivers tested registering above the legal limit of 50 mg/100 ml. The mean BAC of those apprehended through random testing was 99 mg/100 ml, while those apprehended through investigation of traffic

offences had a mean BAC of 130 mg/100 ml, and those apprehended
through their involvement in accidents had a mean BAC of 160
mg/100 ml. See L. Goldberg, 'Random Breath Testing in Sweden,' in
L. Goldberg, ed., *Alcohol, Drugs and Traffic Safety: Proceedings of the
Eighth International Conference on Alcohol, Drugs and Traffic Safety*
(Stockholm: Almqvist and Wiksell, 1981) 846 at 853, 851.

277 Ross, *Deterring the Drinking Driver* 17.
278 H.L. Ross, 'The Scandinavian Myth: The Effectiveness of Drinking-
and-Driving Legislation in Sweden and Norway' (1975) 4 *Journal of
Legal Studies* 285 at 298.
279 Ibid., 309.
280 John Snortum describes such research: 'By widening the methodological net to an eclectic mixture of circumstantial evidence,
opinion data, correlational analysis, and cross-national comparisons,
the case for the controllability of alcohol impaired driving becomes
still stronger. Unfortunately, the causes also become more obscure,
the interactions more complex and the interpretations more subjective. Whatever the cause may be, there seems to be a smaller proportion of alcohol impaired drivers on the road in Norway and Sweden
than in the United States: 'Controlling the Alcohol-Impaired Driver
in Scandinavia and the United States: Simple Deterrence and Beyond'
(1984) 12 *Journal of Criminal Justice* 131 at 145.
281 On the role of factors not captured in a traditional deterrence model
in the income taxation field, see N. Brooks and A.N. Doob in M.L.
Friedland, ed., *Securing Compliance: Seven Case Studies* (Toronto:
University of Toronto Press, 1990) 120–64; K. Smith and K. Kinsey,
'Understanding Taxpaying Behavior: A Conceptual Framework with
Implications for Research' (1987) 21 *Law and Society Review* 639; J.
Carroll, 'Compliance with the Law: A Decision-Making Approach to
Tax Paying' (1987) 11 *Law and Human Behavior* 319.
282 G.E. Tufts and W.T. Beckett, 'The Administrative Sanction Counter-
measure to Impaired Driving' *Fourth Canadian Multidisciplinary Road
Safety Conference* 251.
283 R. Bonnie, 'The Efficacy of Law as a Paternalistic Instrument,' *Nebraska Symposium on Motivation* (Lincoln: University of Nebraska, 1985)
131.
284 J. Haskins and T. Haskins, 'Major Social Action Groups against
Drunken Drivers' *Journal of Studies on Alcohol* Supp. 10 (July 1985)

192; S. Ungerleider and S. Bloch, 'Perceived Effectiveness of Drinking-Driving Countermeasures: An Evaluation of MADD' (1988) 49 *Journal of Alcohol Studies* 191.

285 See, generally, J. Andenaes, *Punishment and Deterrence* (Ann Arbor: University of Michigan Press, 1974).

286 Drunk driving and high accident frequency may be part of a high-risk deviant life-style. One Massachusetts study indicated that over half of drunk driving offenders had previously been arraigned for non-traffic criminal offences: M. Argeriou et al., 'Criminality among Individuals Arraigned for Drinking and Driving in Massachusetts' (1985) 46 *Journal of Studies on Alcohol* 525. Another study has revealed that alcohol consumption over the past seven days was the best predictor of self-reported drunk driving and that dislike of increased enforcement of drunk driving laws was the best attitudinal predictor: R. Wilson and B. Jonah, 'Identifying Impaired Drivers among the General Driving Population' (1985) 46 *Journal of Studies on Alcohol* 531.

In a study of young male drivers, anthropologist Pierre Maranda found a correlation between several measures of life-style and accident experience. Young men with no accidents had self-images of men approximately ten to fifteen years older, while those with accidents had short-term perspectives and craved immediacy of pleasure in many aspects of their lives: P. Maranda, 'An Anthropological View of Sanctions and Rewards,' in M.L. Friedland, ed., *Sanctions and Rewards in the Legal System: A Multidisciplinary Approach* (Toronto: University of Toronto Press, 1989) 166–72.

Andenaes has suggested that motorists with serious alcohol problems or other social shortcomings 'are poor targets for the deterrent and moral effects of the law': J. Andenaes, 'The Scandinavian Experience,' in Laurence et al., eds., *Social Control* 59.

287 Gusfield challenges the relevance of a rationalistic model of decision-making and argues that 'the imagery of deliberation, discussion and resolution implied by [the use of the term *decision*] is not necessarily nor usually appropriate in describing the phenomena' of drinking and driving. See Gusfield et al., 'The Social Control of Drinking-Driving: An Ethnographic Study of Bar Settings' (1984) 6 *Law and Policy* 45 at 46. See also E. Vingilis and R. Mann, 'Toward an Interactionist Approach to Drinking-Driving Behaviour: Implications and Research' (1986) 1 no. 4 *Health Education Research* 273.

288 See R. Kraakman, 'Gatekeeper Liability' (1986) 2 *Journal of Law, Economics and Organization* 53; C.D. Stone, 'Choice of Target and Other Law Enforcement Variables,' in Friedland, ed., *Sanctions and Rewards in the Legal System* 203.

289 J. Little, 'A Theory and Empirical Study of What Deters Drinking and Drivers, If, When and Why!' (1971) 23 *Administrative Law Review* 23 at 41. Based on the results of interviews conducted in the late 1960s, Little found that close to half of a sample allowed a driver who had been drinking to drive and that only a third reported refusing to get into a car with a drinking driver. If social attitudes have changed in ways that reduce drunk driving, then a more recent study should reveal increased willingness to intervene. Some research suggests that the most effective intervention technique is driving intoxicated people home rather than giving them coffee, telling them not to drive, or taking their keys away: see A. Hernandez and J. Rabow, 'Passive and Assertive Student Interventions in Public and Private Drunken Driving Situations' (1987) 48 *Journal of Studies on Alcohol* 269.

290 R. Homel, 'Penalties and the Drunk-Driver: A Study of One Thousand Offenders' (1981) 14 *Australian and New Zealand Journal of Criminology* 225; J.L. Nichols, 'The Effectiveness of Education and Treatment Programs for Drinking Drivers: A Decade of Evaluation,' in L. Goldberg, ed., *Alcohol, Drugs and Traffic Safety: Proceedings of the Eighth International Conference on Alcohol, Drugs and Traffic Safety* (Stockholm: Almqvist and Wiksell, 1981) 1298 at 1311.

291 J. Gusfield, *The Culture of Public Problems: Drinking-Driving and the Symbolic Order* (Chicago: University of Chicago, 1981).

292 A. Donelson et al., *Characteristics of Drinking Drivers* (Ottawa: Department of Justice, 1985) 45. One Australian study found that of 687 drivers involved in fatal accidents in 1977 in Victoria, only 6 per cent had prior drunk driving convictions. Even among those drivers killed in single-vehicle crashes (more likely to involve drunk driving), only 9 per cent had previous drunk driving convictions, although 28 per cent had other previous criminal convictions: J. Hendtlass et al., 'Differences between Drivers Injured and Not Injured in Collisions in Victoria, Australia,' in Goldberg, ed., *Alcohol, Drugs and Traffic Safety*, 124 at 129. A study of impaired drivers responsible for fatal crashes in Alberta similarly revealed that only 11 per cent of those drivers had previous impaired driving convictions: G. Bako et

al., 'Drivers in Alberta with Previous Impaired Driving Records Responsible for Fatal Highway Accidents: A Survey 1970–1972' (1977) 68 *Canadian Journal of Public Health* 106.

293 R. Hagen, 'The Efficacy of Licensing Control as a Countermeasure for Multiple Driving while Impaired Offences' (1978) 10 *Journal of Safety Research* 115.

294 P. Saltzberg and S. Paulsrude, 'An Evaluation of Washington's Driving while Intoxicated Law: Effects on Drunk Driving Recidivism' (1984) 15 *Journal of Safety Research* 117; R. Voas, 'Evaluation of Jail as a Penalty of Drunken Driving' (1986) 2 *Alcohol, Drugs and Driving: Abstracts and Reviews* 47.

295 See chapter 5 below on education.

296 H. Simpson, 'The Epidemiology of Alcohol-Related Accidents,' in P. Noordzij and R. Roszbach, eds., in *Alcohol, Drugs and Traffic Safety: Proceedings of the Tenth International Conference on Drugs, Alcohol and Traffic Safety* (Amsterdam: Excerpta Medica, 1987) 91. The landmark article that brought this insight to light is R. Zylman, 'A Critical Evaluation of the Literature on Alcohol Involvement in Highway Deaths' (1974) 6 *Accident Analysis and Prevention* 163.

297 See discussion above in Introduction. Such environmental features will also counter the danger of a wide variety of driver behaviour, because 'impairments due to drunkenness are not unlike those due to fatigue, absent mindedness, anger ... etc.': M. Moore and D. Gerstein, eds., *Alcohol and Public Policy: Beyond the Shadow of Prohibition* (Washington: National Academy Press, 1981) 101.

298 L. Phillips et al., 'Forecasting Highway Casualties: The British Road Safety Act and a Sense of Déja Vu' (1984) 12 *Journal of Criminal Justice* 101. Such data suggest that traffic safety measures have focused too much on driving behaviour and should take into account environmental design factors, such as roadways and vehicle safety, which can reduce the frequency and severity of automobile accidents.

299 I. Johnston, 'The Potential of Environmental Modification as a Drunk-Driving Countermeasure,' in Noordzij and Roszbach, eds., *Alcohol, Drugs and Traffic Safety* 608–9. See also T. Ranney and V. Gawron, 'The Effects of Pavement Edgelines on Performance in a Driving Simulator under Sober and Alcohol-Dosed Conditions' (1986) 28 *Human Factors* 511.

300 T. Anderson and D. Viano, 'Effects of Acute Alcohol Intoxication on

Injury Tolerance and Outcome,' in Noordzij and Roszbach, eds.,
Alcohol, Drugs and Traffic Safety 251.

301 See Voas, 'Emerging Technologies for Controlling the Drunk Driver,'
in Laurence et al., eds., *Social Control* 334ff. Nine American states
have laws authorizing judges to require ignition interlock devices:
Status Report 24 no. 1 (28 January 1989).

302 See J.L. Mashaw and D.L. Harfst, *Regulating the Freedom Machine*
(Harvard University Press, forthcoming).

303 *Family Law Act*, SO 1986, c. 4, s. 61(2).

304 See R.A. Posner, *Economic Analysis of Law*, 3rd ed. (Boston: Little,
Brown, 1986) 147–51, and A.M. Polinsky, *Introduction to Law and
Economics* (Boston: Little, Brown, 1983) chapter 6.

305 See K.S. Abraham, *Distributing Risk* (New Haven: Yale University
Press, 1986) chapter 2.

306 See, generally, M.J. Trebilcock, 'Incentive Issues in the Design of No-
Fault Compensation Systems' (1989) 39 *University of Toronto Law
Journal* 19; M.J. Trebilcock, 'The Social Insurance-Deterrence Dilemma
of Modern North American Tort Law: A Canadian Perspective on the
Liability Insurance Crisis' (1987) 24 *San Diego Law Review* 929.

307 For a brief review of the history of compulsory automobile insurance,
and its effects on accident rates, see James Foreman-Peck, 'Death on
the Roads: Changing National Responses to Motor Accidents,' in
Theo Barker, ed., *The Economic and Social Effects of the Spread of Motor
Vehicles* (London: Macmillan, 1987) 278–82.

308 For reviews of some of this literature, see S.A. Rea, 'Economic Analysis of Fault and No-Fault Liability Systems' (1987) 12 *Canadian
Business Law Journal* 444; C.J. Bruce, 'The Deterrent Effects of Automobile Insurance and Tort Law: A Study of the Empirical Literature'
(1984) 6 *Law and Policy* 67.

309 E. Landes, 'Insurance, Liability, and Accidents: A Theoretical and
Empirical Investigation of the Effect of No-Fault Accidents' (1982) 25
Journal of Law and Economics 49.

310 See also R. Grayston, 'Deterrrence in Automobile Liability Insurance
– The Empirical Evidence' (1973) 20 *Insurance Counsel Journal* 117.

311 See J. O'Connell and S. Levmore, 'A Reply to Landes: A Faulty Study
of No-Fault's Effect on Fault' (1983) 48 *Missouri Law Review* 649; P.
Zador and A. Lund, 'Re-analyses of the Effects of No-Fault Auto
Insurance on Fatal Crashes' (1986) 53 *Journal of Risk and Insurance* 226;

S. Sugarman, 'Doing Away with Tort Law' (1985) 73 *California Law Review* 558 at 588–90.

312 Zador and Lund, 'Re-analyses'; P.S. Kochanowski and M.V. Young, 'Deterrent Aspects of No-Fault Automobile Insurance: Some Empirical Findings' (1985) 52 *Journal of Risk and Insurance* 269; US Department of Transportation, *Compensating Auto Accident Victims* (1985), Appendix B.

313 See M.H. Medoff and J.P. Magaddino, 'An Empirical Analysis of No-Fault Insurance' (1982) *Evaluation Review* 373.

314 C. Brown, 'Deterrence in Tort and No-Fault: The New Zealand Experience; (1985) 73 *California Law Review* 976.

315 R.I. McEwin, 'No-Fault and Road Accidents: Some Australasian Evidence,' *Proceedings of the International Insurance Society*, Seoul, July 1987, 185–93.

316 M. Gaudry, 'The Effects on Road Safety of the Compulsory Insurance, Flat Premium Rating and No-Fault Features of the 1978 Quebec Automobile Act,' Appendix to *Report of the Inquiry into Motor Vehicle Accident Compensation in Ontario* (Osborne Report) (Ontario: Queen's Printer, 1988); for a description of the Quebec scheme, see J. O'Connell and C. Tenser, 'North America's Most Ambitious No-Fault Law: Quebec's Auto Insurance Act' (1987) 24 *San Diego Law Review* 917; M. Boyer and G. Dionne, 'Description and Analysis of the Quebec Automobile Insurance Plan' (1987) 13 *Canadian Public Policy* 181.

317 R.A. Devlin, 'Liability versus No-Fault Automobile Insurance Regimes: An Analysis of Quebec's Experience,' Paper presented at Canadian Economics Association Meeting, Windsor, Ontario, 3 June 1988.

318 Ibid., 37.

319 US Department of Transportation, *Driver Behavior and Accident Involvement: Implications for Tort Liability* (1970).

320 Ibid., 9, 98, 99, 189–90. See also W. Haddon and S. Baker, 'Injury Control,' in D.W. Clark and B. MacMahon, eds., *Preventive and Community Medicine* (Boston: Little, Brown, 1981).

321 Norman, *Road Traffic Accidents – Epidemiology, Control and Prevention*, World Health Organization, Public Health Papers, No. 12, 1962, 51.

322 S. Partyka, 'Simple Models of Fatality Trends Using Employment and Population Data' (1984) 16 *Accident Analysis and Prevention* 211; J. Hedlund, R. Arnold, E. Cerrelli, S. Partyka, P. Hoxie, and D. Skinner,

'An Assessment of the 1982 Traffic Fatality Decrease' (1984) 16
Accident Analysis and Prevention 247.

323 D.E. Stewart and R.W. Sanderson, 'The Measurement of Risk on
Canada's Roads and Highways,' in S. Yagar, ed., *Transport Risk
Assessment* (Waterloo: University of Waterloo Press, 1984); Osborne
Report 201–17; M. Wilson and M. Daly, 'Competitiveness, Risk
Taking and Violence: The Young Male Syndrome' (1985) 6 *Ethnology
and Sociology* 59; W. Wiegers, 'The Use of Age, Sex, and Marital Status
as Rating Variables in Automobile Insurance,' (1989) 39 *University of
Toronto Law Journal* 149.

324 Bill 2 (1988).

325 See M. Boyer and G. Dionne, 'Description and Analysis of the Quebec
Automobile Insurance Plan' (1987) 13 *Canadian Public Policy* 181; C.R.
Knoeber, 'Penalties and Compensation for Auto Accidents' (1978) 7
Journal of Legal Studies 263.

326 See Osborne Report 530–43.

326a See the Report of the Ontario Automobile Insurance Board dated
July 14, 1989, *Re an Examination of threshold no fault and choice no fault
systems of privately delivered automobile insurance.* The report's Execu-
tive Summary states at p.45: 'The Board is of the opinion that the
proposed systems and in particular the choice system, will result in
an increased accident frequency.'

327 For US law on crashworthiness, see L.R. Frumer and M.I. Friedman,
Products Liability (New York: Matthew Bender, 1960), vol. I, chapter 2,
597, and vol. II, chapter 3, 633.

328 See G.L. Reed, 'Transportation Liability and Risk Management,' in
J.F. Carney, ed., *Effectiveness of Highway Safety Improvements* (New
York: American Society of Civil Engineers, 1986) 92; G.L.G. Hinge,
'Tort Liability in the Pennsylvania Department of Transportation,'
ibid., 102; J.D. Blasche, J.M. Mason, and B.E. Miller, 'Risk Manage-
ment to Reduce Highway Tort Liability,' ibid., 117.

329 See, generally, J.B. Jacobs, 'The Impact of Insurance and Civil Law
Sanctions on Drunk Driving,' in M.D. Laurence, J.R. Snortum, and
F.E. Zimring, eds., *Social Control of the Drinking Driver* (Chicago:
University of Chicago Press, 1988) 227. J.B. Jacobs, *Drunk Driving: An
American Dilemma* (University of Chicago Press, 1989) chapter 10.

330 See G. Sharpe, *The Law and Medicine in Canada*, 2d ed. (Toronto:
Butterworths, 1987), and E.I. Picard, *Legal Liability of Doctors and
Hospitals in Canada*, 2d ed. (Toronto: Carswell, 1984).

331 O'Donnell surveyed eleven studies of the drinking locations of alcohol-impaired drivers and concluded that in these studies 'licensed premises were identified by 40 to 63% of the drivers arrested for drunk driving, 43 to 64 % of the roadside-survey participants with a BAC > .10, and 26% of the accident-involved drinking drivers': M. O'Donnell, 'Research on Drinking Locations of Alcohol-Impaired Drivers: Implications for Prevention Policies' (1985) 6 *Journal of Public Health Policy* 510 at 514–15.

332 See, generally, D. Bedard, 'One More for the Road: Civil Liability of Licensees and Social Hosts for Furnishing Alcoholic Beverages to Minors' (1979) 59 *Boston University Law Review* 725; J. Mosher, 'Dram-Shop Liability and the Prevention of Alcohol Related Problems' (1979) 40 *Journal of Studies on Alcohol* 773.

333 Survey research suggests that the most effective intervention technique is to drive intoxicated people home rather than giving them coffee, telling them not to drive, or taking their keys away. A social host would be in a better position to drive guests home than would be a commercial vendor: A Hernadez et al., 'Passive and Assertive Student Interventions in Public and Private Drunken Driving Situations' (1987) 48 *Journal of Studies on Alcohol* 269.

334 Social host liability has been abrogated by legislation in many states (see Jacobs, 'The Impact of Insurance') and was rejected by a recent Ontario Advisory Committee: S. Offer, *Report of the Advisory Committee on Liquor Regulation* (Toronto: Ontario Queen's Printer, 1987) 92.

335 See V. Aubert, *In Search of Law: Sociological Approaches to Law* (Oxford: Martin Robertson, 1983), and 'On Methods of Legal Influence,' in S.B. Burman and B.E. Harrell-Bond, eds., *The Imposition of Law* (New York: Academic Press, 1979); A. Freiberg, 'Reward, Law and Power: Toward a Jurisprudence of the Carrot' (1986) 19 *Australia New Zealand Journal of Criminology* 91 at 107–11.

336 N. Macchiavelli, *The Prince* (New York: Mentor Books, 1952) 98, cited in Aubert, *In Search of Law* 51.

337 J. Bentham, *Of Laws in General*, H.L.A. Hart, ed. (London: Athlone Press, 1970) 135.

338 Ibid.

339 As a reason for not using a reward-based system of compliance, Bentham cited 'the boundless expense it would require, and the absolute want of a fund from which that expense could be supplied': ibid., 289. Blackstone also considered that the state lacked the resour-

ces for rewarding all law-abiding behaviour: 'Were the exercise of every virtue to be enforced by the proposal of particular rewards, it were impossible for any state to furnish stock enough for so profuse a bounty': see Sir William Blackstone, *Commentaries on the Laws of England* (Dublin: John Exshaw, 1771) 56. See also Aubert, *In Search of Law* 53.

340 C.A. Reich, 'The New Property' (1964) 73 *Yale Law Journal* 733. See also Aubert, 'Methods' 30.

341 See M.L. Friedland, *The Case of Valentine Shortis* (Toronto: University of Toronto Press, 1986) 205; Friedland, 'Sentencing Structure in Canada: Historical Perspectives,' background paper to Report of the Canadian Sentencing Commission, Department of Justice, Ottawa, 1988, section 5(b).

342 Robert Clarke of Harvard Law School discusses techniques used by religions in 'Law Markets and Morals,' a Legal Theory Workshop presentation at the University of Toronto, 22 January 1988.

343 See Hugh J. Arnold, 'Sanctions and Rewards: An Organizational Perspective,' in M.L. Friedland, ed., *Sanctions and Rewards in the Legal System: A Multidisciplinary Approach* (Toronto: University of Toronto Press, 1989) 137.

344 R. Anderson, 'Incentives Tied to Performance Best to Keep Motivation Strong,' *Globe and Mail*, 10 March 1987.

345 *Globe and Mail*, 15 May 1986 and 31 March 1987. The federal government also provides bonuses to its employees for facility in both official languages: ibid., 28 May 1987.

346 L. Martin, 'Radical Wage Reforms Link Pay, Performance to Spur Soviet Workers,' *Globe and Mail*, 10 November 1986.

347 See, for example, a discussion of the use of grants, loans, and tax incentives in the United States to encourage effective management of hazardous wastes, in R.G. Gordon, 'Legal Incentives: A New Approach to Hazardous Waste Management' (1986) 95 *Yale Law Journal* 830. See also W.J. Baumol and E.S. Mills, 'A New Strategy for Toxic Waste: Paying Companies to Obey the Law' *New York Times*, 27 October 1985. On use of grant programs in regulating water pollution, see J.C. Buresh, 'State and Federal Land Use Regulation: An Application to Groundwater and Nonpoint Source Pollution Control' (1986) 95 *Yale Law Journal* 1433 at 1435–6 and 1457.

348 Encouragement of research through the Canadian tax system, however, has led to serious abuses: see *Globe and Mail*, 15 November 1986.

349 See M. Heumann and T.W. Church, 'Criminal Justice Reform, Monetary Incentives, and Policy Evaluation,' paper delivered at the Annual Law and Society Association Meeting, Vail, Colorado, June 1988:
'The results of these incentive-linked innovations are ambiguous.'

350 J. Andenaes, *Punishment and Deterrence* (Ann Arbor: University of
Michigan Press, 1974) 187–8.

351 Aubert, *In Search of Law* 165.

352 A.J. Reiss, 'Selecting Strategies of Social Control over Organizational
Life,' in K. Hawkins and J.M. Thomas, *Enforcing Regulation* (Boston:
Kluwer-Nijhoff, 1984) 23 at 24.

353 See H.J. Arnold, 'Sanctions and Rewards: An Organizational Perspective,' in Friedland, ed., *Sanctions and Rewards in the Legal System*
147–8. See also J. Sheldon, 'How to Set up a Safety Incentive Program'
(1986) 2 *Occupational Health and Safety Canada* 28.

354 *Globe and Mail*, 17 May 1988.

355 Sheldon, 'How to Set up a Safety Incentive Program' 28. And see the
success of the ten-year program in mines using a token economy in
which miners were given redeemable tokens for not having accidents
or injuries for specified periods of time: D.K. Fox, B.L. Hopkins, and
A.K. Anger, 'The Long-Term Effects of a Token Economy on Safety
Performance in Open-Pit Mining' (1987) 20 *Journal of Applied Behavior
Analysis* 215.

356 See *Globe and Mail*, 30 December 1985. See also D. Beirness and M.
Vogel-Sprott, 'Alcohol Tolerance in Social Drinkers: Operant and
Classical Conditioning Effects' (1984) 84 *Psychopharmocology* 393, and
R.E. Mann and M. Vogel-Sprott, 'Control of Alcohol Tolerance by
Reinforcement in Non-alcoholics' (1981) 75 *Psychopharmocology* 315.

357 T.G. Ison, 'The Significance of Experience Rating' (1986) 24 *Osgoode
Hall Law Journal* 723 at 726. See also Ison, 'The Therapeutic Significance of Compensation Structures' (1986) 64 *Canadian Bar Review*
605 at 613.

358 G.J.S. Wilde and P.A. Murdoch, 'Incentive Systems for Accident-Free
and Violation-Free Driving in the General Population' (1982) 25
Ergonomics 879 at 887–8. On the theory of cognitive dissonance, Wilde
refers to L. Festinger, *Conflict, Decision and Dissonance* (Stanford:
Stanford University Press, 1964). See also Wilde, 'The Use of Incen-
tives for the Promotion of Accident-Free Driving' (1985) 46 Suppl 10
Journal of Studies on Alcohol 161; Wilde, 'Beyond the Concept of Risk
Homeostasis: Suggestions for Research and Application towards the

Prevention of Accidents and Lifestyle-Related Disease' (1986) 18 *Accident Analysis and Prevention* 377 at 388ff.

359 E.S. Geller, 'Large Scale Application of Behavior Analysis to Make a Difference' (1985) *Proceedings,* American Psychological Association, Division 23, Consumer Psychology, 3. Geller refers to B.F. Skinner, *Beyond Freedom and Dignity* (New York: Knopf, 1971). In *Science and Human Behavior* (New York: MacMillan, 1953) as well, Skinner argues that government could control behaviour more effectively through positive reinforcement than with punishment: see J.E. Grusec, 'Sanctions and Rewards: The Approach of Psychology,' in Friedland, ed., *Sanctions and Rewards in the Legal System* 108.

360 Unpublished address delivered at a Traffic Injuries Research Foundation Conference, in Edmonton, Alberta, in July 1986. See also Geller, 'Large Scale Application,' and E.S. Geller, 'A Delayed Reward Strategy for Large-Scale Motivation of Safety Belt Use: A Test of Long-Term Impact' (1984) 16 *Accident Analysis and Prevention* 457; E.S. Geller, *Motivating Safety Belt Use with Incentives* (1984), SAE Technical Paper Series; E.S. Geller, 'Rewarding Safety Belt Use at an Industrial Setting' (1983) 16 *Journal of Applied Behavior Analysis* 189; E.S. Geller, G.R. Lehman, M.J. Kalshner, and F.M. Streff, *Long-Term Effects of Employer-Based Programs to Motivate Safety Belt Use,* US Department of Transportation, NHTSA, Report No. DOT HS 807 111, February 1987. See also H. Kunreuther, 'Incentives for Improving Driver Behavior: Ex Ante/Ex Post Considerations,' in L. Evans and R.C. Schwing, eds., *Human Behavior and Traffic Safety* (New York: Plenum Press, 1985) 365 at 372.

361 Geller, 'Large Scale Application.'

362 J.G. Cope, W.F. Grossnickle, and E.S. Geller, 'An Evaluation of Three Corporate Strategies for Safety Belt Use Promotion' (1986) 18 *Accident Analysis and Prevention* 243 at 250.

363 R.J. Bonnie, 'The Efficacy of Law as a Paternalistic Instrument,' in G.B. Melton, ed., *Nebraska Symposium on Motivation, 1985: The Law as a Behavioral Instrument* (Lincoln: University of Nebraska Press, 1986), 131 at 190. See also Cope, Grossnickle, and Geller, 'Evaluation' 243.

364 See E.S. Geller, J.R. Rudd, M.J. Kasher, F.M. Streff, and G.R. Lehman, 'Employer-Based Programs to Motivate Safety Belt Use: A Review of Short-Term and Long-Term Effects' (1987) 18 *Journal of Safety Research*

1; Cope, Grossnickle, and Geller, 'Evaluation' 243. Analysis of
educational programs is discussed below.
365 Cope, Grossnickle, and Geller, 'Evaluation' 250.
366 Geller et al., 'Employer-Based Programs' 14.
367 Ibid., 15.
368 See J. Lacey, speaking in panel discussion reported at (1985) 46, Suppl
10, *Journal of Studies on Alcohol* 168.
369 See discussion of seat-belt use above, in chapter 1.
370 *Status Report* 21 no. 6 (17 May 1986) 7.
371 G.J.S. Wilde and P.A. Murdoch, 'Incentive Systems for Accident-Free
and Violation-Free Driving in a General Population' (1982) 25 *Ergonomics* 879 at 884–5. Wilde distinguishes between incentives announced in advance and rewards that are given unexpectedly after
the fact.
372 See Bonnie, 'The Efficacy of Law' 188. The report is R. Harano and
D.E. Hubert, *An Evaluation of California's 'Good Driver' Incentive
Program*, California Division of Highways, Report No. 6, Sacramento,
1974.
373 Wilde distinguishes between the two experiments in that the second
used incentives and the first ex post facto rewards, but, as stated in
the text, both are incentives. See Wilde and Murdoch, 'Incentive
Systems' 484–5. See also Wilde, 'The Use of Incentives' 164; Bonnie,
'The Efficacy of Law' 188–9.
374 Wilde, 'The Use of Incentives' 164-5; see also Bonnie 'The Efficacy of
Law' 189.
375 Ontario Task Force on Insurance (D.W. Slater, chair), *Final Report*,
Ontario Government, May 1986.
376 Ibid., 120.
377 See the discussion of the effect of Quebec's no-fault scheme on
accidents in the chapter on civil liability and insurance, above. See
also M. Boyer and G. Dionne, 'Description and Analysis of the
Quebec Automobile Insurance Plan' (1987) 13 *Canadian Public Policy*
181.
378 For a recent, somewhat pessimistic review of incentives for safe
driving, compare A.C. Donelson and D.R. Mayhew, *Driver Improvement as Post-Licensing Control: The State of Knowledge* (Ontario Ministry
of Transportation and Communications, 1987) 107–21. The report
concluded (121) that the literature on rewards does 'not offer clear

directions for the development of nonpunitive approaches to driver improvement' but stated: 'Nonetheless, the possibility that nonpunitive programs can improve driving performance among some subgroups of drivers remains.'

379 Wilde, 'The Use of Incentives' 166; Bonnie, 'The Efficacy of Law' 191–2.

380 On the need for controlled experiments, see Kunreuther, 'Incentives for Improving Driver Behavior' 376.

381 G. Williams, 'Control By Licensing' (1967) 20 *Current Legal Problems* 81. For example, in some North American jurisdictions a driver's licence can be temporarily suspended for driving with blood alcohol levels lower than those prohibited by criminal sanctions: see, e.g., Motor Vehicle Act, RSBC 1979, c. 288, s. 214; Highway Traffic Act, SO 1981, c. 72, s. 30(a); Motor Vehicle Administration Act, RSA 1980, c. M-22, s. 110. Probationary conditions can also be placed on newly licensed drivers so that interventions will be imposed earlier in response to traffic violations or accidents.

382 A. Burg, 'Vision and Driving' (1971) 13 *Human Factors* 79 at 83. The results of Burg's multiple regression analysis indicate that personal characteristics such as age, prior conviction experience, and annual distance driven are far better predictors of accident experience than the results of even complex vision tests. In the early 1960s, over two million drivers in Pennsylvania were given physical examinations as a condition of licence renewal. Only 1.7 per cent of those tested were determined to be physically unacceptable as drivers, and this group of drivers had about one-half the accident rate of the average Pennsylvania driver. See National Highway Safety Administration, 'Licensing Conditions Requiring Physicians to Report' (1972) 1 *Traffic Laws Commentary* 10. Furthermore, medical studies had found no correlation between responsibility for fatal crashes and evidence of disease or physical disability. Older drivers do, however, have decreased ability to survive traffic accidents: S. Baker and W. Spitz, 'Age Effects and Autopsy Evidence of Disease in Fatally Injured Drivers' (1970) 214 *Journal of American Medical Association* 1079.

383 See for example, S. Kelsey et al., 'License Extensions for Clean Record Drivers: A Four Year Follow Up' (1985) 16 *Journal of Safety Research* 149; D. Zaidel and I. Hocherman, 'License Renewal for Older Drivers: The Effects of Medical and Vision Tests' (1986) 17 *Journal of Safety Research* 111.

384 On the basis of their multiple regression analysis, Saffer and Grossman estimate that a policy that would have fixed the American federal beer tax in real terms since 1951 and that taxed the alcohol in beer at the same rate as alcohol in liquor would have reduced fatalities amongst eighteen- to twenty-year-olds by 54 per cent between 1975 and 1981. Beer prices would also have increased by approximately 60 per cent. See H. Saffer and M. Grossman, 'Beer Taxes, The Legal Drinking Age and Youth Motor Vehicle Fatalities' (1987) 16 *Journal of Legal Studies* 351 at 372. See also P. Cook, 'The Effect of Liquor Taxes on Drinking, Cirrhosis and Auto Accidents,' in M. Moore and D. Gerstein, eds., *Alcohol and Public Policy: Beyond the Shadow of Prohibition* (Washington, DC: National Academy Press, 1981) 255; J. Mosher, 'Tax-Deductible Alcohol: An Issue of Public Health Policy and Prevention Strategy' (1983) 7 *Journal of Health, Politics, Policy and the Law* 855. On the relation between macro-economic performance and traffic accidents see the chapter on economic variables below.

385 R. Peck et al., 'The Distribution and Prediction of Driver Accident Frequencies' (1970) 2 *Accident Analysis and Prevention* 243 at 267.

386 Studies in Ontario have indicated that drivers with large numbers of convictions and demerit points have significantly higher accident rates but also suggest that many of these drivers do not have higher accident rates when their increased driving exposure is taken into account. See M. Chipman and P. Morgan, 'The Predictive Value of Driver Demerit Points' *Proceedings of the American Association for Automotive Medicine* (1974) 399; M. Chipman and P. Morgan, 'The Driver Demerit Point System in Ontario as a Long-Term Predictor of Collisions' in *Proceedings of the American Association for Automotive Medicine* (1976) 45; M. Chipman, 'The Role of Exposure, Experience and Demerit Point Levels in the Risk of Collision' (1982) 14 *Accident Analysis and Prevention* 475.

387 L. Robertson and S. Baker, 'Prior Violation Records of 1,447 Drivers Involved in Fatal Crashes' (1975) 7 *Accident Analysis and Prevention* 121 at 122–3.

388 R.C. Peck et al., 'The Distribution and Prediction of Driver Accident Frequencies' (1970) 2 *Accident Analysis and Prevention* 243 at 272. Likewise, Burg, in a study of California drivers, concluded that if all drivers with one or more accidents in a three-year period were removed from the road, 19.8 per cent of all drivers would be re-

moved in order to eliminate 29.6 per cent of accidents over the second three-year period. If only drivers with two or more accidents were removed, 3.9 per cent of all drivers would be taken off the road to eliminate 8.0 per cent of all accidents over the next three years; if all drivers with three or more accidents were removed, only 0.08 per cent of drivers would be affected but only 2 per cent of accidents would be prevented. See A. Burg, 'The Stability of Driving Record over Time' (1970) 2 *Accident Analysis and Prevention* 57 at 63. These calculations are based on the assumption that no driving will occur during the period of suspension, whereas it is known that many, perhaps most, drivers with suspended licences continue to drive.

389 R. Zylman, 'Drivers' Records: Are They a Valid Measure of Driving Behaviour?' (1972) 4 *Accident Analysis and Prevention* 333; see also Transport Canada Road Safety Report, *Effectiveness of Traffic Law Enforcement*, TP 1662, undated, probably 1973.

390 R. Peck, 'Toward a Dynamic System of Driver Improvement Program Evaluation' (1976) 18 *Human Factors* 493 at 497, 499.

391 See B.A. Jonah, 'Accident Risk and Risk-Taking Behaviour among Young Drivers' (1986) 18 *Accident Analysis and Prevention* 255; R. Naatanen and H. Summala, *Road-User Behavior and Traffic Accidents* (Amsterdam: North-Holland, 1976) 91–9, on the role that young drivers' desires and perceptions of risk play in traffic accidents. See D. Stewart and R. Sanderson, 'The Measurement of Risk on Canada's Roads and Highways,' in S. Yagar, ed., *Transport Risk Assessment* (Waterloo: University of Waterloo Press, 1984) 12, on the disproportionate accident risk of both young drivers and inexperienced drivers with less than eleven years of driving experience.

392 P. Cook and G. Tauchen, 'The Effect of Minimum Drinking Age Legislation on Youthful Auto Fatalities, 1970–1977' (1984) 13 *Journal of Legal Studies* 169 at 171; see also P. Whitehead et al., 'Collision Behavior of Young Drivers: Impact of the Change in the Age of Majority' (1975) 36 *Journal of Studies of Alcohol* 1208; G. Bako et al., 'The Effect of Legislated Lowering of the Drinking Age on Fatal Highway Accidents among Young Drivers in Alberta' (1976) 67 *Canadian Journal of Public Health* 161; C. Liban et al., 'The Canadian Drinking-Driving Countermeasure Experience' (1987) 19 *Accident Analysis and Prevention* 159 at 169ff. See, generally, A. Wagenaar, *Alcohol, Young Drivers and Traffic Accidents* (Lexington: D.C. Heath, 1983).

393 A. Williams et al., 'The Effect of Raising the Minimum Driving Age on Involvement in Fatal Crashes' (1983) 12 *Journal of Legal Studies* 169 at 176.

394 W. DuMouchel et al., 'Raising the Alcohol Purchase Age: Its Effects on Fatal Motor Vehicle Crashes in Twenty-Six States' (1987) 16 *Journal of Legal Studies* 249 at 254.

395 H. Saffer and M. Grossman, 'Beer Taxes, the Legal Drinking Age and Youth Motor Vehicle Fatalities' (1987) 16 *Journal of Legal Studies* 351 at 373.

396 E. Vingilis and R. Smart, 'Effects of Raising the Legal Drinking Age in Ontario' (1981) 76 *British Journal of Addiction* 415 at 420ff.

397 A. Wagenaar, 'Raised Legal Drinking Age and Automobile Crashes: A Review of the Literature' (1982) 3 *Abstracts and Reviews in Alcohol and Driving* 3 at 5.

398 M. Males, 'The Minimum Purchase Age for Alcohol and Young-Driver Fatal Crashes: A Long Term View' (1986) 15 *Journal of Legal Studies* 181.

399 E. Vingilis and K. DeGenova, 'Youth and the Forbidden Fruit: Experiences with Changes in Legal Drinking Age in North America' (1984) 12 *Journal of Criminal Justice* 161 at 164.

400 A. Williams, 'Comment on Males' (1986) 15 *Journal of Legal Studies* 213; W. DuMouchel et al., 'Raising the Alcohol Purchase Age: Its Effects on Fatal Motor Vehicle Crashes in Twenty-Six States' (1987) 16 *Journal of Legal Studies* 249 at 250–1.

401 Richard Bonnie suggests: 'Underage drinkers probably drink less frequently than they would if alcohol were commonly and readily available to them and they are far less likely to be drinking in on premise locations, where the age restriction is most easily enforced. Thus, the legal restrictions at least pushes aggregate behavior in the desired direction.' See R. Bonnie, 'The Efficacy of Law as a Paternalistic Instrument' (1985) *Nebraska Symposium on Motivation* 149–50.

402 See, generally, M. Moore and D. Gerstein, eds., *Alcohol and Public Policy: Beyond the Shadow of Prohibition* (Washington, DC: National Academy Press, 1981). Regulation through liquor licensing laws and 'dram shop' civil liability is directed toward the behaviour of commercial servers of alcohol, but little is known concerning the effects and potential of such regulation on the drinking driving problem. See discussion above on sanctions and drunk driving.
Some form of restricting availability of alcohol may have dysfunc-

tional effects. One study has found a significant inverse correlation between traffic fatalities and the number of licensed premises per capita, suggesting that drinking and driving may increase if people must travel longer distances to buy alcohol. See I. Colon and H. Cutter, 'The Relationship of Beer Consumption and State Alcohol and Motor Vehicle Policies to Fatal Accidents' (1983) 14 *Journal of Safety Research* 83; I. Colon, 'County-Level Prohibition and Alcohol-Related Fatal Motor Vehicle Accidents' (1983) 14 *Journal of Safety Research* 101. Closing hours might have negative effects on traffic safety by forcing patrons to vacate bars and seek transportation while their blood alcohol levels are still rising.

403 A. Williams et al., 'Variations in Minimum Licensing Age and Fatal Motor Vehicle Crashes' (1983) 73 *American Journal of Public Health* 1401. The researchers did not believe that the offsetting effects were so great as to cancel completely reductions in sixteen-year-old driver fatalities attributed to the raised minimum age.

404 P. Gorys, *Preliminary Evaluation of the Probationary Driver Program in Ontario* (Toronto: Ontario Ministry of Transport and Communications, 1983) vii. In 1981 Ontario introduced a probationary driver program; drivers in their first two years of licensing would have their licence suspended (and their probationary period begin anew) upon accumulation of only six demerit points, as opposed to the fifteen-point limit for regular drivers. During the program's first year of operation, drivers subject to it had 9 per cent fewer accidents and 14 per cent fewer convictions than similar drivers in a control group examined before implementation of the program. A follow-up study suggested that probationary drivers had fewer accidents over their first two years of driving but also that some of the reductions could be attributed to reductions in the accident rates of the overall population: R. Rosenbaum et al., 'Ontario's Probationary Driver Program: Continuing Evaluation' in *Fourth Canadian Multidisciplinary Road Safety Conference* (Montreal, 1988) 499.

405 See, generally, D.R. Mayhew and H.M. Simpson, *Graduated Licensing: State of Knowledge and Current Practices* (Ottawa: Traffic Injury Research Foundation of Canada, 1984).

406 D.F. Preusser et al., 'The Effect of Curfew Laws on Motor Vehicle Crashes' (1984) 6 *Law and Policy* 115.

407 A.J. McKnight et al., *Youth License Control Demonstration Project*

(Washington, DC: NHTSA, 1984) as reported in Mayhew and Simpson, *Graduated Licensing* 62.

408 L. Robertson, 'Patterns of Teenaged Driver Involvement in Fatal Motor Crashes: Implications for Policy Choice' (1981) 6 *Journal of Health Politics, Policy, and Law* 303 at 309–10.

409 See H.L. Ross and P. Gonzales, 'Effects of License Revocation on Drunk-Driving Offenders' (1988) 20 *Accident Analysis and Prevention* 379.

410 R. McBride and R. Peck, 'Modifying Negligent Driving Behavior through Warning Letters' (1970) 2 *Accident Analysis and Prevention* 147; A. Donelson and D. Mayhew, *Driver Improvement as Post-Licensing Control: The State of the Knowledge* (Toronto: Ministry of Transportation and Communication, 1987) 33ff. McBride and Peck's study found warning letters to be slightly more effective in reducing accidents than traffic violations. The authors note, however, that the consensus of research suggests that driver improvement interventions 'have demonstrated a greater capacity for reducing violations than accidents' and that traffic violations are generally 'a much more stable and sensitive index of driving behavior than accidents': ibid., 173.

411 Specific examples are discussed below in chapter 5.

412 R. Williams et al., 'A Driving Record Analysis of Suspension and Revocation Effects on the Drinking-Driving Offender' (1984) 16 *Accident Analysis and Prevention* 333 at 333; see also R. Hagen et al., 'The Efficacy of Licensing Controls as a Countermeasure for Multiple D.W.I. Offenders' (1978) 10 *Journal of Safety Research* 115; B. Jones, 'Oregon's Habitual Traffic Offender Program: An Evaluation of the Effectiveness of License Revocation' (1987) 18 *Journal of Safety Research* 19. In the latter study, those who received notice of their licence suspension had 1.8 accidents per 100 drivers, while a similar group who received a second warning letter had 4.8 accidents per 100 drivers.

413 The results of interviews with convicted drunk drivers who have had their licences suspended suggest that drivers both reduce their driving activity and when driving perceive a high risk of apprehension and exercise greater caution so as to avoid detection: see E. Wells Parker and P. Cosby, 'Behavioral and Employment Consequences of Driver's License Suspension for Drinking Driving Of-

fenders' (1988) 19 *Journal of Safety Research* 5 at 15ff; H.L. Ross and P. Gonzales, 'Effects of License Revocation on Drunk-Driving Offenders' (1988) 20 *Accident Analysis and Prevention* 379.

414 Donelson and Mayhew, *Driver Improvement* 98–100.
415 A. McKnight and M. Edwards, 'A Taste of Suspension: The Preventive and Deterrent Value of Limited License Suspension' *American Association for Automotive Medicine Proceedings* (1987) 45.
416 R. Hagen et al., 'The Traffic Safety Impact of Alcohol Abuse Treatment as an Alternative to Mandated Licensing Controls' (1979) 11 *Accident Analysis and Prevention* 275; R. Williams et al., 'A Driving Record Analysis of Suspension and Revocation Effects on the Drinking-Driving Offender' (1984) 16 *Accident Analysis and Prevention* 333; R. Peck et al., 'The Comparative Effectiveness of Alcohol Rehabilitation and Licensing Control Actions for Drunk Driving Offenders: A Review of the Literature' (1985) 1 *Alcohol, Drugs and Driving: Abstracts and Reviews* 15.
417 J. Shaoul, *The Use of Accidents and Traffic Offenses as Criteria for Evaluating Courses in Driver Education* (Salford: University of Salford Press, 1975), described in L. Robertson, *Injuries* (Lexington: D.C. Heath, 1983), 92ff.
418 L. Robertson and P. Zador, 'Driver Education and Fatal Crash Involvement of Teenaged Drivers' (1978) 68 *American Journal of Public Health* 959.
419 L. Robertson, 'Crash Involvement of Teenaged Drivers when Driver Education Is Eliminated from High School' (1980) 70 *American Journal of Public Health* 599.
420 Robertson and Zador, 'Driver Education' 959; A. Lund et al., 'High School Driver Education: Further Evaluation of the DeKalb County Study' (1986) 18 *Accident Analysis and Prevention* 349. As Lund et al. have concluded: 'If driver education has provided any additional crash avoidance skills, they have been inadequate to compensate for the licensure effect': ibid., 349.
421 C.J. Helander, 'Intervention Strategies for Accident-Involved Drivers: An Experimental Evaluation of Current California Policy and Alternatives' (1984) 15 *Journal of Safety Research* 23. This California study found an approximately 20 per cent reduction in accidents after either licensing re-examination, a short driver improvement course, or a mailing of educational material.
422 A. Lund and A. Williams, 'A Review of the Literature Evaluating the

Defensive Driving Course' (1985) 17 *Accident Analysis and Prevention* 449.

423 F. McGuire, 'The Effectiveness of a Treatment Program for the Alcohol-Involved Driver' (1978) 5 *American Journal of Drug and Alcohol Abuse* 517.

424 J. Nichols et al., 'The Specific Deterrent Effect of ASAP Education and Rehabilitation Programs' (1978) 10 *Journal of Safety Research* 177. R. Mann et al. report several additional studies in which drunk driving offenders exposed to these short-term 'Phoenix-style' educational programs have had fewer drunk driving arrests than those who received no education: Mann et al., 'Programs to Change Individual Behaviour: Education and Rehabilitation in the Prevention of Drinking and Driving,' in M. Laurence, J. Snortum, and F. Zimring, eds., *The Social Control of the Drinking Driver* (Chicago: Chicago University Press, 1988) 261ff.

425 M. Anderson and P. Merrick, 'Dunedin Course for Impaired Drivers: A Model for New Zealand?' (1980) 13 *Australia and New Zealand Journal of Criminology* 133 at 138.

426 R. Holden, 'Rehabilitative Sanctions for Drunk Driving: An Experimental Evaluation' (1983) 20 *Journal of Research in Crime and Delinquency* 55. Both these latter studies may, however, reflect difficulties in achieving random assignment to treatment and control groups because judges are reluctant to assign those whom they perceive as having the worse problem to a no-treatment control group. For example, in the New Zealand study, judges tended to assign those with higher BACs at arrest and more previous drunk driving convictions to the treatment group that received education.

427 E. Vingilis et al., 'The Oshawa Impaired Drivers Programme: An Evaluation of a Rehabilitation Programme' (1981) 23 *Canadian Journal of Criminology* 93 at 97ff.

428 Mann et al., 'Programs to Change Individual Behavior' 265.

429 D. Preusser et al., 'Driver Record Evaluation of a Drinking Driving Rehabilitation Program' (1976) 8 *Journal of Safety Research* 98; R. Peck et al., 'The Comparative Effectiveness of Alcohol Rehabilitation and Licensing Control Actions for Drunk Driving Offenders: A Review of the literature' (1985) 1 *Alcohol, Drugs and Driving: Abstracts and Reviews* 15.

430 Mann et al., 'Programs to Change Individual Behaviour' 261.

431 E. Geller et al., 'Employer-Based Programs to Motivate Safety Belt

Use: A Review of Short Term and Long Term Effects' (1987) 18
Journal of Safety Research 1; J. Cope et al., 'An Evaluation of Three
Corporate Strategies for Safety Belt Use Promotion' (1986) 18 *Accident
Analysis and Prevention* 43.

432 F. Seixas and A. Hopson, 'The Effect of Rehabilitation on the Driving
Behaviour of Problem Drinkers,' in S. Israelstram and S. Lambert,
eds., *Alcohol, Drugs and Traffic Safety: Proceedings of the Sixth International Conference on Alcohol, Drugs and Traffic Safety* (Toronto: Addiction Research Foundation, 1975) 723.

433 R. Mann et al., 'School-Based Programmes for the Prevention of
Drinking and Driving: Issues and Results' (1986) 18 *Accident Analysis
and Prevention* 325.

434 L. Robertson et al. found that a television campaign involving 943
showings of commercials over a nine-month period had no observable effect on safety belt use, as compared to a similar control group,
which did not receive the messages through cable television: L.
Robertson et al., 'A Controlled Study of the Effect of Television
Messages on Safety Belt Use' (1974) 64 *American Journal of Public
Health* 1071 at 1077ff.

435 R. Smart and R. Cutler, 'The Alcohol Advertising Ban in British
Columbia: Problems and Effects on Beverage Consumption' (1976) 71
British Journal of Addictions 13; P. Kohn and R. Smart, 'The Impact of
Television Advertising on Alcohol Consumption' (1984) 45 *Journal of
Studies on Alcohol* 295. In the latter controlled experiment, exposure to
commercials increased beer consumption over the first thirty min-
utes, but further exposure to advertising did not significantly affect
consumption.

436 An Arizona study, however, suggested that publicity that preceded
passage of new drunk driving legislation may have been more
important in deterring drunk driving and reducing alcohol-related
accidents than actual passage of legislation: T. Epperlein, 'Initial
Deterrent Effects of the Crackdown on Drinking Drivers in the State
of Arizona' (1987) 19 *Accident Analysis and Prevention* 285.

437 P. Farmer, 'The Edmonton Study: A Pilot Project to Demonstrate the
Effectiveness of a Public Information Campaign on the Subject of
Drinking and Driving,' in Israelstam and Lambert, eds., *Alcohol,
Drugs and Traffic Safety* 831 at 838. Information campaigns should not
concentrate on conveying information that is of little practical use,
such as prohibited BAC levels. For example, publicity in Britain was

able to have only 29 per cent of respondents know the illegal BAC level, but 99 per cent knew that alcohol could be detected by means of a breath test and 95 per cent knew that they could not refuse a breath test: NHTSA, *Alcohol and Traffic Safety 1984: A Review of the State of the Knowledge* (Washington, DC: NHTSA, 1984) 77.

One commentator has suggested that rather than try to raise unrealistic fears of the likelihood of punishment or to change attitudes and morals, publicity campaigns will be most effective if they provide practical information to help individuals avoid 'driving when dangerously or illegally drunk': D. Reed, 'Reducing the Costs of Drinking and Driving,' in M. Moore and D. Gerstein, eds., *Alcohol and Public Policy: Beyond the Shadow of Prohibition* (Washington, DC: National Academy Press, 1981) 336.

438 MADD *Newsletter*, fall 1985, 13: 'Lightner also publicly expressed shock and dismay at a holiday public awareness campaign sponsored by Ireland's National Road Safety Organization. The campaign "only two will do" encourages Irish citizens to limit their alcohol intake to "only" two drinks before driving. She stressed that you do not have to be legally intoxicated to kill or injure innocent victims – only impaired – and two drinks will definitely place drivers at the point of impairment.'

439 In a recent Canadian survey, over 75 per cent of adults interviewed drank alcohol on a regular basis, and of this group 50 per cent reported driving after drinking, with 14 per cent admitting that they drove while they thought they were legally impaired: R.J. Wilson, *A National Household Survey on Drinking and Driving: Knowledge, Attitudes and Behaviour of Canadian Drivers* (Ottawa: Transport Canada, 1984) ii.

440 On the importance of publicity, see generally H.L. Ross, *Deterring the Drinking Driver*, revised ed. (Lexington: D.C. Heath, 1984) chapters 4 and 5. Ross (69–70) notes that the most effective enforcement campaigns are those that are 'more controversial, more publicized and more newsworthy.' See also G. Mercer, 'The Relationships among Driving while Impaired Charges, Police Drinking-Driving Roadcheck Activity, Media Coverage and Alcohol-Related Casualty Traffic Accidents' (1985) 17 *Accident Analysis and Prevention* 467. Mercer demonstrated that a measure of publicity in the form of the amount of newspaper coverage of enforcement activities is a better predictor of reductions in alcohol-related accidents than the amount either of charges laid or of drivers stopped.

441 National Research Council, *Injury in America* (Washington, DC: National Academy Press, 1985) 38.

442 See L. Evans, 'Driver Behavior Revealed in Relations Involving Car Mass,' in L. Evans and R.C. Schwing, eds., *Human Behavior and Traffic Safety* (New York: Plenum Press, 1985) 337, and literature cited therein.

443 S. Partyka, 'Simple Models of Fatality Trends Using Employment and Population Data' (1984) 16 *Accident Analysis and Prevention* 211.

444 J. Hedlund, R. Arnold, E. Cerelli, S. Partyka, P. Hoxie and D. Skinner, 'An Assessment of the 1982 Traffic Fatality Decrease' (1984) 16 *Accident Analysis and Prevention* 247.

445 J.H. Hedlund, 'Recent U.S. Traffic Fatality Trends,' in Evans and Schwing, eds., *Human Behavior and Traffic Safety* 7.

446 Ibid., 17.

447 J.G.U. Adams, *Risk and Freedom: The Record of Road Safety Regulation* (Cardiff: Transport Publicity Projects, 1985) 140.

448 Hedlund, 'Recent U.S. Traffic Fatality Trends,' 9, 10.

449 See, generally, G.W. Trinca et al., *Reducing Traffic Injury: A Global Challenge* (Melbourne: Royal Australasian College of Surgeons, 1988) 64–5.

450 See G. Calabresi, *The Costs of Accidents* (New Haven: Yale University Press, 1970).

451 H. Saffer and M. Grossman, 'Beer Taxes, the Legal Drinking Age, and Youth Motor Vehicle Fatalities' (1987) 16 *Journal of Legal Studies* 351. This study is supported by others that suggest that restrictions on availability of alcohol through increases in prices or in the minimum legal drinking age are related to reductions in alcohol consumption and that levels of alcohol consumption in turn are related to levels of alcohol-related traffic accidents. See D. Coate and M. Grossman, 'Effects of Alcoholic Beverage Prices and Legal Drinking Ages on Youth Alcohol Use' (1988) 21 *Journal of Law and Economics* 145; R. Mann and L. Anglin, 'The Relationship between Alcohol-Related Traffic Fatalities and per Capita Consumption of Alcohol, Ontario, 1957–1983' (1988) 20 *Accident Analysis and Prevention* 441.

452 See J. Foreman-Peck, 'Death on the Roads: Changing National Responses to Motor Accidents,' in Theo Barker, ed., *The Economic and Social Effects of the Spread of Motor Vehicles* (London: MacMillan, 1987) 280.

453 See J.W. Eastman, *Styling versus Safety* (Lanham, Md: University Press of America, 1984); A. Irwin, *Risk and the Control of Technology* (Manchester: Manchester University Press, 1985) chapters 4 and 5.

454 R. Nader, *Unsafe at Any Speed: The Designed-In Dangers of the American Automobile* (New York: Grossman, 1965).

455 See J.L. Mashaw and D.L. Harfst, 'Regulation and Legal Culture: The Case of Motor Vehicle Safety' (1987) 4 *Yale Journal of Regulation* 257; Mashaw and Harfst, *Regulating the Freedom Machine* (Harvard University Press, forthcoming); Eastman, *Styling versus Safety*. See Introduction to this study.

456 Mashaw and Harfst, *Regulating the Freedom Machine* chapter 3.

457 National Traffic and Motor Vehicle Safety Act, Pub. No. 89-563, 80 Stat. 718 (1967), codified as amended at 15 USC 1381–1431 (1982).

458 Motor Vehicle Safety Act, RSC 1970, 1st suppl., c. 26.

459 R.W. Crandall, H.K. Gruenspecht, T.E. Keeler, and L.B. Lave, *Regulating the Automobile* (Washington, DC: Brookings Institution, 1986) 51.

460 Discussed in J. Claybrook and D. Bollier, 'The Hidden Benefits of Regulation: Disclosing the Auto Safety Payoff' (1985) 3 *Yale Journal of Regulation* 87.

461 Cited in Crandall et al., *Regulating the Automobile* 51–5.

462 Claybrook and Bollier, 'Hidden Benefits' 87, 88.

463 Ibid., 93.

464 Mashaw and Harfst, 'Regulation.'

465 Ibid., 313.

466 S. Peltzman, 'The Effects of Automobile Safety Regulation' (1975) 83 *Journal of Political Economy* 677.

467 Ibid., 682.

468 L.S. Robertson, 'A Critical Analysis of Peltzman's "The Effects of Automobile Safety Regulation"' (1977) 11 *Journal of Economic Issues* 587.

469 L.C. Orr, 'The Effectiveness of Automobile Safety Regulation: Evidence from the FARS Data' (1984) *American Journal of Public Health* 1384.

470 Crandall et al., *Regulating the Automobile*.

471 Ibid., 81–4.

472 G. Blomquist, *The Regulation of Motor Vehicle and Traffic Safety* (Washington, DC: American Enterprise Institute, 1987) chapter 4.

473 See, above, on seat-belt use in chapter 1.

474 Crandall et al., *Regulating the Automobile* 69.
475 For alternative perspectives on this issue, see the special issue, *Risk* (1986) 18 *Accident Analysis and Prevention*.
476 Ibid., 367–75.
477 See Mashaw and Harfst, *Regulating the Freedom Machine*.
478 See, generally, Adams, *Risk and Freedom*.
479 Ibid., 140.
480 Ibid., 141–3; see also G.J.S. Wilde, 'Beyond the Concept of Risk Homeostasis: Suggestions for Research and Application toward the Prevention of Accidents and Lifestyle-Related Disease' (1986) 18 *Accident Analysis and Prevention* 393–5.
481 S. Peltzman, 'The Effects of Automobile Safety Regulation' (1975) 83 *Journal of Political Economy* 689.
482 G.M. MacKay, *A Review of Road Accident Research* (Birmingham: Department of Transportation and Environmental Planning, University of Birmingham Press, 1962).
483 See, e.g., W. Haddon and S.P. Baker, 'Injury Control,' in D.W. Clark and B. MacMahon, eds., *Preventive and Community Medicine* 2d ed. (Boston: Little, Brown, 1981).
484 K.C. Sinha and K. Hu, 'Assessment of Safety Impacts of Highway Projects,' in J.F. Carney, ed., *Effectiveness of Highway Safety Improvements* (New York: American Society of Civil Engineering, 1986) 31. For a detailed review of research on highway safety design, see US Department of Transportation, Federal Highway Administration, *Synthesis of Safety Research Related to Traffic Control and Highway Elements*, 2 vols. (1982); see also OECD, *Road Safety Research: A Synthesis* (Paris, 1986), chapter 12.
485 E. Hauer, 'The Reign of Ignorance in Road Safety: A Case for Separating Evaluation from Implementation,' Conference on Transportation Deregulation and Safety, Northwestern University, June 1987; Hauer, 'A Case for Science-Based Road Safety Design and Management,' Safety Studies Group, Department of Civil Engineering, University of Toronto, 1988.
486 See also Foreman-Peck, 'Death on the Roads' 270–3.
487 Hauer, 'A Case for Science-Based Road Safety Design' 3.
488 R.C. Bennett, 'Economic Analysis of Highway Safety Projects,' in Carney, ed., *Effectiveness* 147.
489 E. Hauer, 'Review of Published Evidence on the Safety Effect of Conversion from Two-Way to Four-Way Stop Sign Control,' Working

Paper, University of Toronto, Department of Civil Engineering, 1985; G.M. Ebbecke, 'An Examination of the Areawide Effects of Traffic Control Device Installation in a Dense Urban Area,' Department of Civil Engineering, Villanova University, May 1976.

490 S.R. Lynch, 'Location and Development of Safety Projects,' in Carney, ed., *Effectiveness* 80–5; M.J. Stelzleni, 'Benefit-Cost Analysis of Highway Safety Improvements,' in Carney, ed., *Effectiveness* 152–8.

491 Bennett, 'Economic Analysis.'

492 R.W. Lyles and A.G. Drakopoulos, 'Some Questions on the Accuracy of Safety Effectiveness Evaluations,' in Carney, ed., *Effectiveness* 172–9.

493 E. Hauer, 'Selection for Treatment as a Source of Bias in Before-and-after Studies' (1980) *Traffic Engineering and Control* 419–21; see also C. Abbess, D. Jarrett, and C.C. Wright, 'Accidents at Blackspots: Estimating the Effectiveness of Remedial Treatment with Special Reference to the "Regression-to-Mean" Effect' (1981) *Traffic Engineering and Control* 535–42.

494 Hauer, 'Review.'

495 G.M. Ebbecke and J.J. Shuster, 'Areawide Impact of Traffic Control Devices,' in *Transportation Research Board Record* (Washington, DC: Transportation Research Board, 1977) 644.

496 C.C. Wright and A.J. Boyle, 'Accident "Migration" after Remedial Treatment at Accident Blackspots' (1984) *Traffic Engineering and Control* 260–6.

497 R.G. Smith and A. Lovegrove, 'Danger Compensation Effects of Stop Signs at Intersections' (1983) 15 *Accident Analysis and Prevention* 95.

498 Adams, *Risk and Freedom* chapter 4.

499 Ibid., 43.

500 Ibid., 44.

501 Ibid., 45.

502 Ibid., 48.

503 Ibid., 22, 23.

504 Crandall et al., *Regulating the Automobile.*

505 See, generally, Trinca et al., *Reducing Traffic Injury* 72–74, 102–5.

506 D.D. Trunkey, 'Trauma' (1983) 249 *Scientific American* 28 at 34.

507 C. Gardner, 'Emergency Care of the Crash Injury Victim,' *Proceedings of the Montreal Conference on the Medical Aspects of Traffic Accidents,* ed. H. Elliott (Montreal: Sun Life Assurance Co. of Canada, 1955); Trunkey, 'Trauma' 33, 34.

508 H. Mitchell, *Emergency Medical Care and Traffic Fatalities* (Santa Monica, Calif.: Rand Corp., 1968).

509 F. Van Wagoner, 'Died in Hospital: A Three-Year Study of Deaths Following Trauma' (1961) 1 *Journal of Trauma* 401.

510 S.R. Shackford, P. Hollingworth-Fridlund, G. Cooper, and A. Eastman, 'The Effect of Regionalization upon the Quality of Trauma Care as Assessed by Concurrent Audit before and after Institution of a Trauma System' (1986) 26 *Journal of Trauma* 812.

511 Trunkey, 'Trauma' 33.

512 Shackford et al., 'Regionalization.'

513 Trunkey, 'Trauma' 32, 33.

514 Ibid., 34.

515 US Department of Transportation, *Compensating Auto Accident Victims* (1985) 107–12.

516 Ibid.

517 See, e.g., T.G. Ison, 'The Therapeutic Significance of Compensation Structures' (1986) 64 *Canadian Bar Review* 605; Trunkey, 'Trauma' 35.

518 Ison, 'Significance' 622.

519 *Compensating Auto Accident Victims* at pp. 79-81.

520 J. Henle, *Rehabilitation of Auto Accident Victims*, US Department of Transportation Automobile Insurance and Compensation Study 13 (1970), 18–19.

521 Ison, 'Significance.'

522 J. Dooley, 'Psychological Impact of Chronic Pain and Disability Resulting from Motor Vehicle Accidents,' in *Crash Injury, Impairment and Disability: Long Term Effects*, International Congress and Exposition Proceedings, Society of Automotive Engineers, Detroit, Michigan, 1986, 81 at 84.

523 The US experience in the early 1970s with the ignition interlock design requirements to ensure seat-belt usage, for example, brought forth such vehement public reaction that the regulation had to be dropped: see Mashaw and Harfst, *Regulating the Freedom Machine*.

524 For evidence of major disparities in expenditures on life-saving counter-measures, see J.F. Morrall, 'A Review of the Record' (1986) November/December *Regulation* 25.

525 Statistics on gun use have been taken from 'Gun Control in Canada: Politics and Impact,' in M.L. Friedland, *A Century of Criminal Justice: Perspectives on the Development of Canadian Law* (Toronto: Carswell, 1984) 113ff. See also J.H. Sloan et al., 'Handgun Regulations, Crime,

Assaults, and Homicide: A Tale of Two Cities' (1988) 319 *New England Journal of Medicine* 1256, which examines handgun use and regulations in Seattle, Washington, and in Vancouver, British Columbia, and concludes (1261): 'Our analysis of the rates of homicide in these two largely similar cities suggests that the modest restriction of citizens' access to firearms (especially handguns) is associated with lower rates of homicide. This association does not appear to be explained by differences between the communities in aggressiveness, criminal behavior, or response to crime. Although our findings should be corroborated in other settings, our results suggest that a more restrictive approach to handgun control may decrease national homicide rates.'